Playthings Past

For my husband Christopher, with love and thanks for shared enthusiasm, and for the young at heart – everywhere.

Playthings Past

Betty Cadbury

David & Charles
Newton Abbot   London   Vancouver

ISBN 0 7153 7191 6

Set in 10 on 11 pt Times Roman
and printed in Great Britain
for David & Charles (Publishers) Limited
Brunel House Newton Abbot Devon

Published in Canada
by Douglas David & Charles Limited
1875 Welch Street North Vancouver BC

Acknowledgements

Many people help to write a book and no one learns more than the author. Thanks are due to correspondents who answered queries, to museum officials and to commercial firms who supplied information from their archives. The author gratefully acknowledges permission to reprint extracts from her articles in the Antique Collectors' Club Journal and the Doll Club of Washington's souvenir booklet.

Sincere thanks are tendered to Mr C. C. Manley for sharing his knowledge of the glass-making industry, to Mary Hoxie Jones for compiling the history of the Cadbury dolls in America and to Joyce Banks for preparing the bibliography.

Especially the author thanks Hugh Miles, whose excellent photographs illustrate the text, and Margaret Palmer who typed it so thoughtfully. All the items illustrated are in the author's collection except the Cadbury dolls, some Micromodels, the Meccano set and the engraving by John Burnet (Optical Toys); for the loan of the latter, the writer is indebted to the Trustees of the Winds Point Trust.

Research is a lengthy process and no one could be more grateful than the author for the understanding and co-operation from her family. Above all, she remembers generations of children whose make-believe world made this book possible.

Contents

Introduction

The aim of this book is to give the interested reader and collector some knowledge of the scope of yesterday's toys. In no way is it a comprehensive list of toys – this can be obtained by studying old and new toyshop catalogues. Fortunately, such is the loyalty and inbred tradition of children that many games and toys survive to this day in various forms little altered from the original. Like Mother's favourite recipes, they were 'handed down'. Thank goodness.

Many of the toys mentioned here can be studied in specialist books. People have written knowledgeably on children's literature, dolls, toy soldiers, etc and a glance at the bibliography will be a useful guide to further study. However, a collector needs a book which gives some indication of the scope of the subject and this I have aimed to do. Its many imperfections will be remedied by students and researchers in their own fields and in their own good time; slowly, perhaps, if they are diverted by the temptation to amuse themselves with the fascinating items which they discover.

I believe that illustrations provide the easiest method of identification and so there are many pictures and these, perhaps, seen through twentieth-century eyes, may evoke the nostalgia which prompts the thought 'I had one of those – where is it now?'.

Toys to amuse were and still are found in most societies, eg a ball made and bound with rushes, a dolly of corn stalks, loose hoops from a barrel. For poor families, toys were an unknown luxury; only wealthy families could employ craftsmen. Then came the industrial revolution, increased wages and mass-production. Toy-making and toy-owning had arrived.

To collect antique and period toys is a challenge. The very early ones are almost unobtainable and the collectable items, therefore, must lie between the late Georgian and Edwardian eras, giving a span of about 150 years. The early toys – since those times were urgent, hard and a matter of survival – must surely have been those that taught, rather than those that amused; a band of toy soldiers that could aid battle instruction – a doll to assist in nursery training – beads to teach numbers – a moral book, rather than a story book. This type of toy was almost universal and its descendant is the educational toy of today. Toys, therefore, were made to instruct, to amuse and, later, to sell to a steadily expanding market. And this is where one begins to collect. Although poorer Victorian families could afford only the necessities of life, the middle and upper classes furnished their nurseries with all manner of exciting, novel and well-made toys, many designed to amuse and instruct. The Victorian home was very much the centre of family life and consequently many toys provided entertainment for the whole household and not exclusively for the child, eg the magic lantern, the Zoetrope or Wheel of Life. Pastimes, too, enabled education and amusement to be combined, notably craftwork using shells, beads, feathers, hair, cut paper, etc. The child completing a dissected puzzle (so called until the use of the jigsaw), making a scrap-book or stitching a sampler, trained eyes, fingers, brain and patience at the same time.

The word 'toy' can mean a small object or can describe a method of passing the time; thus the exquisite silver miniatures, some of the intricate automata and the steel toy which stands on the executive's desk of today are, strictly speaking, adult playthings. One must always remember that the life of a toy was never meant to include its eventual display in a museum – 200 years later. It was intended to do no more than give its owner a span of amusement or instruction. The fact that so many enchanting examples have survived to be collected is an indication of good manufacture and care of possession, rare in today's toy owners who have greater purchasing power and indestructible plastics to make them less careful of preservation.

Although there are specialists in the field of antique toy collecting and many museums in Britain and America show folk collections, the subject has only recently become generally popular. American toys are a study in themselves and unique in many respects, particularly in the field of bell and cast-iron toys.

The lack of a specific catalogue class is demonstrated by the fact that some salerooms include toys in their sales of watches, clocks, rugs and carpets! So the search is spread over a wide field. The information given here is an attempt to survey some of the toys which should be included in a representative collection and apologies are tendered in advance for all those favourites which have been omitted!

Improvised Toys

The paintings and drawings of child subjects and family groups over at least the last two centuries show us not only authentic details of costume but also how many and varied were the toys they enjoyed: ivory and coral rattles with bells, dolls, whipping tops, hoops, baby houses, hobby-horses, rocking horses, push-and-pull toys and wheeled toys (prams, carts, etc).

But only the children of comfortably-off people had their portraits painted or their photographs taken. In the 1870s there would have been a great difference in the toys of the agricultural labourer and those of the factory worker. When children were sometimes kept from school because they had no boots, there were few pennies to spare for toys. Many had only the simplest – a home-made rag doll, a cheap toy from the annual fair or the travelling pedlar, or one given in exchange by the rag-and-bone man.

Necessity is the mother of invention and improvised toys are worth studying and collecting. Allied to the fact that a poor child had to make his own toys was the feeling of pride in achievement and the enjoyment of making something out of nothing. Boys probably whittled away with penknives, fashioning toy boats to sail in stream or gutter, or a windmill to turn in the breeze, and what boy has not contrived devastating toys with elastic bands, Y-shaped twigs and paper pellets? If they were fortunate enough to own a fretsaw, all sorts of things were possible.

Girls used their skills in needlework to make rag dolls, items for their dolls' houses, or 'pretend' shops with tiny scraps of

Above
A teaspoon representing a doll. Sticks are sewn into the bodice sleeves and black lace over a scrap of worn satin is used for the skirt.
Victorian/English/Length: 5½in
At right, a clever adaptation of a clay pipe. The base of the bowl is painted to represent a face with black hair and prominent nose. The stem of the pipe fits into a reel of thread hidden beneath the skirt. The flannel petticoat is the needle-book and hanging from the waist is a tiny black bag filled with shoe buttons. A card written in minute letters and attached to the waist reads:

'My name is Miss Piper
I'm not a pen-wiper,
But if my wares you daily use
You'll keep the buttons on your shoes.'

c 1825/English/Height: 7in

Above
A stamp snake (child-made). The stamps are threaded on to a cord, and the brown velvet head has beads for eyes and a mouth lined with red felt. All the corners have been cut from the stamps to make the rounded body of the snake.
c 1870/English/Length: 29in

A life-size frog made of cotton wool, carefully modelled and painted. The eyes are seeds.

c 1900/English/Length: 3½in

material begged from drapers' stores. Such things as old spoons, clothes pegs, potatoes, straw, matchboxes and fir-cones could be transformed by any imaginative child. What better hobby-horse than a broom-handle with a duster for a head?

Adults too were fervent improvisers. Father made models of cathedrals painstakingly constructed of thousands of matchsticks glued together, or converted orange boxes into dolls' houses and shoe boxes into dolls' cradles. Mother collected shells, dried seaweed and other unlikely materials to make toys for her children, or to sell at charity bazaars.

The Victorian period was a great age for doing things at home. Waste of any kind meant hardship for poor households and was disapproved even by richer ones.

Patrick Murray, in the introduction to his book *Toys*, mentions the improvised toys of slumland, 'the ill-tied bundles of rag, paper and bone made by the children themselves'. These home-made specimens must surely be the basis of any collection. Whereas those of a poor child would have been made from discarded items, children from better-off homes were encouraged to use good materials and received help from governess or parents in making finished toys which were of some excellence and by no means cheap to produce. Thus there are several types of improvised toys for the collector to search for, including those made very skilfully by adults – and they will be priced accordingly.

To give an idea of the variety of toys which could be improvised, here are some items which were described in R. K. & M. I. R. Polkinghorne's book *Toy-Making in School & Home* published in 1917: matchbox toys: cork, cardboard and paper toys: merry-go-rounds: swinging boats: gondolas and birds: fire engines: gypsy caravans: swinging and jointed animals: crane: windmills: dancing clown: rocking animals: kites: trellis toys. This is only a selection from a fascinating list.

Dolls' house items were often improvised. Beds (particularly four-posters) and cradles seem to have been home-made in many dolls' houses where the rest of the furniture was commercially made. Ladies' journals and children's magazines frequently gave advice to the maker of miniature items and of course all the soft furnishings, such as bed linen and curtains, were hand made.

The essence of true improvised toys is the use of easily available or discarded materials and a good imagination. Victorian children used shells, feathers, straw, beads and seaweed. In America, dolls' heads were realistically contrived from sculpted and dried apples. These were particularly successful when a brown or lined face was desired, such as a pedlar woman's or an Indian's.

Children today can more easily find plastic bottles or cardboard tubes from throw-away paper rolls but they too will fashion imaginative toys, and collectors of the future can only wait to see what this generation will produce.

Far left

A rare doll of fine white kid with painted features and fur wig. Dressed in white pantaloons and mauve silk dress and wrapped round with the original note, which reads: 'Doll made and dressed for Esther Mary Benson by her mother as she reclined on the sofa during her confinement'.

It is dated the 7th month 1824. Height: 4in

A home-made chest of drawers made from six matchboxes fitted into a wooden frame. The 'handles' are buttons and the castors are jet beads.

c 1910/English/Size: 4½ x 3½ x 3½ in

Left

Two souvenir dolls (male and female) made of seaweed.

Victorian/Foreign/Height: 5in

A set of dolls' house furniture made from corks, pins, cretonne and Macramé string. The note with the suite reads: 'Made by a sailor in Sick Bay, so that he could have a little extra money for 'smokes.' He lost both legs in action and his life in a fire from which it was not possible to rescue him'.

c 1917/English/Height: 1½in

Left
A wooden spoon doll, the bowl painted to represent a face. All the clothes are household cloths, dusters etc, the greying hair is a scrubbing brush, the 'bonnet' a sink mop. This type of doll was commonly dressed by ladies for sale at bazaars. Round the waist is the original card, which reads:

An Experienced General
You stir your porridge with my face,
And with my apron dust the place.
The dishes wash up with my shawl,
It's very strong though very small.
My skirt you'll say is not a 'hobble'
'Twill clean your floors without much
    trouble.
And if you want a mop, it's said
You'll find it on my wooden head.
Just take me as I here appear
You'll find me useful and not dear.
My hair is really turning grey
Because Lloyd George I must obey.

The reference to Lloyd George is interesting; summer time was introduced by his government in 1916, and added a further inconvenience to the domestic servant's life since she was now struggling in near darkness to prepare the house before the family rose in the morning.

c 1917/English/Height: 17in

Above right
A home-made doll of crepe paper representing an elegant lady with flounced dress, muff and hat. The hair is of black wool and the face of white cartridge paper with painted features. The limbs are padded beneath the paper and the dress is sewn with sequins and tiny paper flowers.

Mid-20th century/English/Height: 12in

Above left
An example of adult craftwork. Forty peach stones representing a variety of small objects (squirrel, basket, jug etc) are carved, smoothed and varnished, and the collection is mounted on a home-made standing shield.

c 1910/English

13

Paper Toys

Hand-made paper was too expensive to be used without care, a fact demonstrated by the personal letters of earlier times when clear, uniform writing in one direction was overwritten with lines in the opposite direction – both equally legible.

Not only children delight in handling paper. The Victorian lady made elaborate paper flowers and used rolled and gilded paper to ornament boxes and cabinets. To-day paper is cheap. Street entertainers fold and tear newspaper and it is shredded, soaked and glued to make all sorts of papier-mâché toys – masks, dolls' heads, puppets etc. Paper has a universal appeal and a special place in the history of toy-making.

Machine-made paper and lithography brought a great variety of toys onto the market. From the paper Pantins – cut-out figures with threaded limbs which were popular in France in the mid-eighteenth century – developed the cut-out sheets of paper dolls and other novelties for which the Pellerin family became so famous.

Tableaux or panoramas were another paper toy popular in the nineteenth century. They could reach astonishing lengths – twenty feet or more – when fully extended and were hand coloured. As the manufacturers stressed 'A few copies are coloured with extra care, mounted on a roller and enclosed in a cylindrical case'.

The French town of Épinal was renowned for its production of images, lithographs and engravings, and the cut-out sheets known as 'Imageries d'Épinal' are collectors' items. Today this type of creative play takes the form of kits for model-making. Amongst the finest of paper card assembly sets were the Micromodels of the 1950s. (See Indoor Games)

The early nineteenth century saw the beginning of the paper-doll dressing games. Percy Muir, in *English Children's Books*, mentions a series of paper-doll books invented by S. and J. Fuller (1810). Each figure had a removable head which fitted into a paper pocket on the back of the figure, and was accompanied by a story in rhyme. Later examples consisted of a one-dimensional doll of card or stiffened paper, with a wardrobe of slip-on dresses and hats to match. Accessories were also included – muffs, furs, parasols and fans. Sometimes

Left

An early and unusual paper toy. It depicts three designs for Paris fashions for 1826 and 1827, and five for regional costumes; all are hand painted. The face portion of the illustrations has been cut away so that each loose leaf can be laid over the master sketch which shows a very pretty face (at left centre of illustration). The whole contained in a folder with marble design paper on the outer cover.

c 1826/French/Size: 4½ x 5in

Right

Maria Taglioni was a celebrated 'danseuse' born in 1804. She made her debut in Paris in 1827 and after a brilliant continental career she died in 1884. This boxed set portrays her with nine costumes and head-dresses. They are exquisitely hand coloured and are made with back and front view; the doll slips between and is inserted head first into the costume skirt. The head-dress fits on to the head, showing the hair. An accompanying printed slip names each opera and describes the individual costumes. The coloured and gilded box is a fine example of artistic presentation. This type of doll dressing set was sold at the *papetier*, or stationer, rather than at a toy shop.

c 1829/1830/French/Size: box 7¾ x 10½in; doll 9¼in

Above

A tableau of the procession at the coronation of Queen Victoria. This panorama toy stretches for 20 feet. It is hand coloured and linen backed and was published in June 1838 by Robert Tyas, of 50, Cheapside, London; it cost 14 shillings.

c 1838/English/Size: covers 8 x 5in; length 20ft.

the figures represented royalty, famous singers or actresses.

The delicate early examples gradually gave way however to cheaper, cruder types, as did the boxed sets of card and paper houses, shops, schools and farms. In the last half of the nineteenth century Germany produced some of the finest boxed sets of paper figures. To a collector, these decorated boxes are almost as desirable as the toy contents.

Paper was a most exciting material for the amateur and the professional toy-maker alike. Provided it was not too thick, it could easily be managed by small fingers. Through imagination and patience it could be transformed into decorations for the Christmas table, gold stars for the tree, scarlet bells and latticed lanterns. It stretched into impromptu fancy dresses of crêpe paper and was used for all manner of colourful wrappings, paper chains and comical masks. Commercially it was used for the delicate lace-paper work of Victorian greeting cards, scraps, swaying mobiles and many assembly toys. And, although the purist may shudder, a toy enthusiast must surely include some examples of those paper items which were collected by children – postcard and stamp albums, matchbox labels, seals, postmarks and autographs.

Paper seems an obvious material for quiet games, seated at the table with scissors and glue, and yet even a brief survey of paper toys would be incomplete if it failed to mention kites. Kite-flying, an ancient and national pastime in the East, was certainly known in pre-Christian times and the gorgeous paper models of birds, flowers, dragons and fish that flash and soar in wind and sky bring paper toy-making to the status of art.

The Japanese are celebrated for origami, the art of paper-folding, and also for their paper fans and water flowers. Who can forget those minute pieces of magic which were emptied into a glass of water and suddenly unfolded into a growing garden of brilliant flowers?

Another delightful paper toy was the story-book with cut-out pictures which could be raised to give the illusion of perspective. These were popular in the mid-nineteenth century. Some examples of that

An early paper game called 'The Auction'. A boxed set of small square cards (1¼in) each printed with a hand-coloured illustration of a household or personal article – a mousetrap, cradle, wig, spy-glass, etc. The box lid shows the auction in progress and the instructions for enacting it are printed in German and French. On the base of the box is inscribed the owner's name and the date – 21 July 1851.

Mid-19th century/German/Size of box: 5½ x 6½in

What a little blackamoor!
What a little grub!
If you want to see him clean
see him in his tub.

Above

A page from a moving picture book. Children's books are a subject in themselves, but some can be classified as paper toys. Typical of this genre were the dissolving picture books, wherein one picture (divided into four) changed into another by means of tabs which were pulled or pushed to effect the change. It seemed almost magical, and accompanying verses helped the game. This picture of a toddler playing with the coals before the fire alters into a view of the same child splashing in a wooden bath on the nursery rug.

(From *Pleasant Surprises for Chicks of all Sizes* published by E. Nister, Nuremberg. There were editions in England and America.)
c 1890s

Top left

A card doll with costumes, named on the reverse 'Lady Margaret' and made by Raphael Tuck & Sons, in their Artistic Series. There are four hats and six dresses – dinner dress, afternoon gown, reception gown, morning costume, ball dress, bridal costume. The dresses are attached by shoulder tabs and the neck-piece slides underneath the chin of the model.

c 1894/English/Size: doll 9¼ high

Bottom left

A boxed paper toy entitled 'A German Hunting Party in the Middle Ages'. The box contains a three-sided background scene of castle and woods with an attached interior paper folder on which is written 'a present on her 7th Birthday from her loving cousins. Dec. 1856'. There are 21 card pieces depicting in bright, glossy colour, scenes and figures full of movement.

Mid-19th century/German/Size: 21 wooden mounts, the largest 9½in the shortest 2¼in period, hand coloured and with parts moved by means of tabs, could give most interesting changes of position and occupation – not always suitable for children.

Dean & Son (England) also made moveable books and produced many other paper toys and dolls. America, however, must be considered one of the foremost producers of paper toys and the collector is most likely to find an example by McLoughlin Brothers, New York. Their early productions date to the last quarter of the nineteenth century, and they produced a great variety of paper toys including miniature furniture and toy soldiers.

Some 200 years ago, diligent ladies designed and made pin-pricked pictures, using different sized pins to give variation and depth and lightly colouring the backgrounds and features of the portraits. The paper had to be laid upon something firm but padded, so that the pins could be easily inserted and withdrawn. If the picture showed a room or indoor scene, the 'lamps' and windows were cleverly pricked out so that the interior

appeared to be illuminated when held to the light. This satisfactory occupation for fireside evenings was quickly taken up by the young, and various publications gave instructions for simple designs – flowers, shells, foreign costumes and designs for scrolls and borders. Children's efforts at pin-pricking were surprisingly accomplished, but, as in the 'samplers' they sewed so carefully, excellence was expected and with time abundantly theirs, it was often achieved. The sewing cards with punched holes on sale today are a development of this early craft.

Dressmakers of the late eighteenth century sometimes drew sketches of the dresses that were ordered, and fitted these by means of tabs onto little hand-drawn and coloured paper mannequins. Thus a dressmaker might send to a client a paper folder containing designs for perhaps eight dresses and hats, including a sketch for one or two fancy dresses or court costumes. These would have been the forerunners of the paper dolls which later inhabited the nursery.

Following this tradition, the English firm of Raphael Tuck & Sons Ltd produced many series of paper dolls and doll-dressing sets. They also published postcards, penny jig-saw puzzles, Valentine and Christmas cards, coloured scraps, panoramas, peepshows and many other paper novelties. Unfortunately the firm's records were lost in wartime bombing; a collection of their paper toys would make a most interesting study for the specialist.

The list of paper toys is extensive, ranging from the elaborate souvenirs of great occasions and famous buildings – the opening of the Thames tunnel, the Great Exhibition of 1851, the Eiffel Tower, coronations and processions etc – to the sheets of coloured scraps and those infuriating transfers which never fulfilled childish expectations!

Collectors will find it hard to acquire paper toys in good condition. Obviously they were fragile, had no appearance of value and were first candidates for the discard pile. They are worth seeking and rank among the most desirable of toys.

Dennison's paper doll fashions. The card dolls are realistically tinted and have coloured socks, shoes and swinging limbs attached by eyelets. Instructions were given for printed patterns which had first to be cut out in cardboard and then in white paper. From these templates, dresses, coats and hats were cut from crêpe paper and fitted onto the different sized dolls. The firm issued paper dolls, costume books for party dresses, animal and bird cut-outs and children's party lines (birthday cards, napkins, bon-bon boxes etc). For Valentine's Day it sold paper hearts, arrows and cupids. It specialised in the use of crêpe paper which could be used either in the sheet or twisted into ropes to make baskets, trays, vases and many other items.

c 1920/American/Size illustrated here: dolls 9¼in, 7½in and 6in

Above
A three-fold screen with scraps on both sides, made and decorated by a child. Victorian scrap-books show that besides commercially produced scraps, greeting cards, labels from pastes and pomades, Sunday school texts and anything else suitable for cutting out were used, pasted into albums with thick embossed covers and strong leaves; they were also pasted onto screens.

Victorian/English/Size: each leaf 12½ x 7in

Top right
Tiny Tots Collapsible Dolls' House. The walls and roof slot together. The floors are printed with carpets and the rooms with mirrors, pictures and doors; the outside walls are decorated with paper balcony and climbing roses in relief. A boxed paper toy of the cheapest kind but very satisfactory.

Early 20th century/English/Size: length 8½in; height 6in; depth 6in

Farmyards were made on the same principle, with animals and milkmaid which fitted into tin clips and could be arranged as desired.

Right
The Animated Nursery. A boxed paper toy with models of 'golly', clown, cat, doll and dog; the platform floor is pressed into position and slots through the walls. The figures have swing limbs and bodies; they are fixed into a wire slide and pushed through an opening at the back so that they can be manipulated to perform on the stage. The background is printed with toy motifs.

Early 20th century/English (Mathews & Co Ltd, Leicester)/Size: 11½ x 9½in; figures 4½in

Models

dolls' houses and furnishings, shops, schools, circuses, kitchens, carriages, arks, soldiers, rocking and wheeled horses.

Dolls' Houses and Furnishings

Many toys were – and are still – models of familiar things, varying in scale but true in detail. This is one of the reasons that old toys appeal to the collector, for not only do they represent objects now vanished from contemporary life, but they also show the changes that have occurred in those still around us. The battlemented fort and the horsedrawn carriage have gone, but the grocer's shop and the train have merely changed their outmoded style for a modern form. The grocer's shop, with its frock-coated salesman, is a far cry from the self-service supermarket – as is the steam train from the diesel locomotive.

Luxury models must have been bought by prosperous families with room enough to house them. Large dolls' houses, rocking-horses, carriages, stables etc could only have been nursery toys for the affluent. The smaller models of shops, schools, forts, circuses, Nativity scenes etc, were produced in various sizes, qualities and materials.

The Dutch made very fine model houses enclosed in expensive cabinets, but these seventeenth-century rarities are mostly in museums. Rare, too, are the early 'baby houses' of the eighteenth century; but happily it is still possible to see and buy delightful dolls' houses of the nineteenth century. The earlier ones usually had their own stands, sometimes with drawer or removable roof for storage of extra furniture. Sometimes they can be found fully furnished; more often the furnishing is absent or incomplete.

Most dolls' houses were made by carpenters working on big estates, or by those commissioned to make a special toy for Christmas or birthday, and many houses have been handed down with the chosen additions of succeeding generations. Hence, the contents of a house do not by any means comprise a certain guide to its age – it could well be furnished with the special favourites of three or more generations. For today's collector of furnishings there is great variation in scale, materials and prices. If one is collecting dolls' houses, as distinct from showing just one as an example of a type of toy, then several smaller houses, offering a wide date range, are more desirable.

The early cabinets were almost certainly

Dolls' house. External features: dormer windows front and back, carved pillars to the front door, and pediment. The front and side doors consist of double opening doors, with door furniture. Each pane of glass is fixed with separate wooden glazing bars, both inside and outside the house. There are thirty-six opening exterior doors and windows. The house, which rests on its own stand, opens by means of hinged partitions. The front and back walls of the house open in proportions of two thirds to one third of the walls.

Internal features: there are thirteen rooms altogether with two landings, main hall, kitchen and study running the full depth of the house. All the rooms are inter-connecting, with sixteen interior doors.

Ground floor: study/library, entrance hall, kitchen.
First floor (front): drawing-room, first landing, dining-room.
First floor (back): music room, maids' bedroom.
Second floor (front): master bedroom, second landing, nursery.
Second floor (back): maids' bedroom, bath/wash room.
The finest feature of this house is the craftsman-made staircase which has carved balusters, treads and curved handrail; the staircase wells are fitted with baluster guards on both landings.

c 1880/English/Size: house 54 x 36½ x 25in; stand 13 x 46½ x 30½in

The contents of this house are not all of one period. Most items were sold commercially and some were hand made. Carpets in dolls' houses were often cut from suitable bits of material such as heavy velvet, felt or plush, but one can find exquisite hand-sewn and embroidered carpets and rugs in the grander houses. Kitchen floors were sometimes painted to imitate flagstones, or left bare. In the house illustrated here there are no pictures, but many old houses show tiny framed photographs or miniature prints (those of royalty being especially popular). Real silver items were usually found only in the more expensive houses and were really 'toys' for grown-ups. Nevertheless some did find their way into dolls' houses. Often it is the outside additions which add particular interest to a house and the collector is especially fortunate to find an attached conservatory, a water pump, or a small scale perambulator waiting beside the front door.

made for the delight of adults and were furnished with expensive trifles, but the houses made for children, although rougher in quality, are the ones a collector looks for today – with or without staircases and mostly without bathrooms! House building nowadays is expensive and many families have to be content with a kitchen, living/dining area and one or two bedrooms. Not so our ancestors, who had very definite ideas about a special room for a specific purpose.

It was normal in some early European houses for the lowest floor of the house to be used for storage, or as stalls for animals; the family lived above. In the eighteenth and nineteenth centuries, households took the opportunity to expand: the era was characterised by gracious living and it was not uncommon to find a house enjoying two kitchens, perhaps a dairy and laundry, a housekeeper's room, a butler's pantry, spacious hall, dining room, withdrawing room, library, writing room, music room, nursery, family bedrooms and servants' quarters.

The elaborate dolls' houses also followed this pattern and, for a toy collector with sufficient space, it is probably more satisfactory to try to find a big, old house, rather than several small ones because so many different items of dolls' house furniture do turn up from time to time.

Dolls' houses vary in size, design and method of opening. The early ones were kept locked and only played with on special occasions. One example is described in detail (page 21) but almost all types of houses were copied in doll-sized miniatures – thatched cottages, baronial halls, castles, villas, town houses, country mansions etc. Not only traditional materials were used, but also card and paper. Present day manufacturers, inspired by past designers, are producing very satisfactory houses of card, complete with cut-out paper furniture (and inhabitants!). One of these should certainly be included in a collection.

Most dolls' house furniture was made from wood or metal. The catalogues of German toy manufacturers of the mid-nineteenth century show ranges of furniture, so mass-production was certainly responsible for most items, but one also finds many

Left

These items show the ingenuity of the makers. The four-poster is of cigar-box wood; the chair to the left, with maid, is of carved horn; the chair with seated doll is of blue and white glass beads strung on wire. In the immediate left foreground are a chair and 'conversation seat' of card and poultry bones (those called wishbone or merrythought). The chair at right foreground is made of feathers, and the lady languishes upon a cardboard sofa.

Victorian taste in household decoration preferred paint that did not shine – shades of Venetian red, chocolate and sage green were popular. Velvet covered chairs were trimmed with fringe and some fireplaces had two pokers – one for use and one to look at!

Victorian/English/Various sizes: four-poster 7½in high; feather chair 3in high

Bottom left

The grate, sold by 'A. Loriot, Toyman, Stationer & Perfumer to the Prince and Princess of Wales, No. 60 New Bond St. London' has a working spit mechanism and drip tray to collect the fat. On the shelf stands a Jersey milk can, salt box and spice rack labelled 'Cayenna, Clovos, Cinnamon.' To the left is a Regency wash-stand, a fitted work-table on a bearskin rug and a meat-roaster with reversible fire-shield. In the right background – a plate-warmer, a curtained tin shower-bath and a rack with decorated wooden plates. In the centre are two knife-boxes, a chamber stick with snuffer attached and a metal screen for 'drawing up' the fire. In the immediate foreground – a bird-cage with parrot and a water-butt with brass taps.

Top right

Services and cutlery; the service is wooden, painted cream and decorated with a flower-sprig pattern. The cutlery and napkin rings are of Britannia metal and not made to the same scale as the service.

c 1890/German/Size: plates 2in diameter; knives 4¼in long

Right

Two bedrooms in a typical late Victorian house, showing maid's room (left) and family bedroom (right). The family bedroom is filled with heavy dark furniture, probably mahogany, but the maid's room is sparsely furnished with white painted wooden bed, chest, chair and washstand. Suitably framed upon the wall would be a few lines relating to conduct and the desirability of punctuality, duty, and thanks for blessings received!

interesting pieces made of unusual materials (see page 22). Home crafts were encouraged and practised with help from the family: cigar-box wood, corks and pins, shells, pigeon feathers, beads, visiting cards, lace and even poultry bones were all used to make miniature reproductions.

In addition to the usual items of household furniture, the collector will seek those extras which turn a house into a home – cutlery, model foods, china, glass, kitchen pots, ornaments, pictures, carpets, candlesticks, tin baths, mirrors etc. Each addition is a triumph, especially if the articles are at all uncommon. The largest range of dolls' house foods was of German manufacture, varying in scale and displayed on platters of china, plaster and even paper with painted rims. There were other ways of obtaining these tempting morsels for the table. 'The Girl's Realm' of 1905 gives illustrations and instructions for making dolls' house dinner services, candlesticks, bottles and plates made from bread pellet which had been hardened, dried and painted. This homely ingredient was also used to make realistic foods – roast chicken, cottage loaves, sausages and hams. Hard to find and much sought after are hanging lighting fixtures, lamps with globes, paper-leaved books, lidded knife boxes, work tables, candleboxes, snuffers, bird cages, etc.

Many collectors agree that the delicately turned and painted wooden services are the most useful for the greatest date-range of houses. Sets of fine bone china and fragile Bristol glass were all made in miniature but are more difficult to acquire. Happily, numbers of coarse white pottery pieces are still available today and, for a toy collector, these are more typical of the limits of Victorian pocket money! Since household items of Britannia metal (an alloy of tin and antimony) were extensively used as respectable substitutes for silver and pewter, it was soon copied in miniature and cutlery, candlesticks, services, coffee and tea pots were all manufactured in dolls' house size.

Furnished dolls' houses, perhaps more than any other toy, mirror the fashions of the age. But whether the model is large or small, expensive or cheap, it was, nevertheless, a replica of something viable in its own time in history. One has only to compare a Regency house with a late Victorian example to see how the elegant style changed to the dark and cluttered interiors of the last half of the nineteenth century; even the social customs were preserved in miniature.

Before World War I, the European manufacture of dolls' house furniture was prolific and differed in quality and price. There were cheaper pieces of whitewood, painted tin, cane and wickerwork. The collector can distinguish the better pieces by their finish and polish. The doors and drawers opened easily and were frequently made to imitate the more expensive woods.

However, a fully furnished dolls' house, although a treasure to own, does not give a collector the same enjoyment as an old empty house which needs to be furnished. A perfectionist will hunt out the old items; a creative owner may prefer to improvise. Many collectors combine the two approaches by finding as many as possible of the original fitments and making careful reproductions to fill the gaps until the right piece comes along. However, installing all these desirable objects still presents a problem. They may be wrong in scale and period compared with the rest of the furnishings.

As a dolls' house collector, this question of scale will worry you. As a collector of children's toys, it should not trouble you unduly. The children who played with these houses cared not a whit and popped in anything they thought appropriate: a monstrous piece of coal in the grate, toys from cosaques (nineteenth-century crackers), a pin-cushion from the sewing basket, a china dog as large as the table – with complete disregard as to whether or not they 'fitted'. Preoccupation with perfection of scale is a grown-up attitude of mind.

Notes for Collectors
Dating The architectural features are not an infallible guide to dating, since many houses were copies of earlier designs. More useful indications of age are locks and stands (both found with early houses), the type of nail used in the construction (hand-made nails were used until about 1840), thin glass, and butterfly hinges.

Lighting This is a personal choice for collec-tors. A purist would not install electricity in an old house. On the other hand, some form of subdued lighting does enable the contents to be seen adequately and certainly gives 'life' to a house. Be careful that heat does not build up inside a closed house, especially if it contains wax items.

A valuable 'find' would be some original small-patterned wallpaper suitable for a dolls' house. Many old houses reappear after many years in attics, damp basements or outhouses, with consequent damage to wall coverings.

Duplicate dolls' house furnishings can be displayed on open shelves, showing either fitments for a specific room, or sets of furniture – chairs, suites etc. Also, a collector should look out for furnished rooms, as distinct from complete houses, and for items of miniature furniture, such as apprentice pieces or other examples of the cabinet-maker's craft.

Just as houses were an obvious choice for the toy-maker to copy from the grown-up world, so also were other institutions of daily life – churches, shops, schools, etc.

Shops
When populations were smaller and more localised, the craftsman could sell his individual work. Then came the markets where increasing numbers could buy and sell. From the markets developed the specialised shops – grocers, butchers, milliners, etc – culminating in the department store where, for the convenience of a more affluent society, all manner of merchandise could be displayed under one roof.

Toy merchandising followed the same progression, the stalls and shops of the Victorian era being the most collectable: the butcher's shop with hanging joints of painted red and white plaster; the milliner's shop with desirable bonnets and shawls are items which the collector will probably have to seek in the salerooms. More likely finds will be models of stalls and booths constructed at home, with wares cut out of card, painted and stuck to the display top. Such labours of home industry, like the pedlar dolls, were preserved beneath glass domes. Shops, on the other hand, were usually marketed toys made of metal or wood and in various sizes. With shelves filled with small moveable goods, counters displaying tiny models and sliding drawers correctly labelled, 'playing shops' must have been an absorbing game. It also perfectly demonstrated that miniature world beloved of children.

The British Toymaker mentioned in its September issue of 1916 a Liverpool firm who made a 'promising line in half-guinea sweetshops'. This was a wooden two-storeyed model with glass windows, bottles of sweets, scales, stationery supplies and imitation money.

The same paper described and illustrated model foods made by the Bestikon Toy Industry of London. It was noted for making 'dessert, breakfast, lunch and dinner sets'. The colouring was 'true to life, hand-done' and 'only non-poisonous harmless colours' were used. 'Each course is stuck firmly on a white plate with decorative blue band' and consisted of six dishes packed in a special box and laid on fancy cut-out tissue paper. The firm also made baskets of strawberries, flower-pots and bunches of flowers. The coloured boxes varied according to contents – dessert service in bright blue box, breakfast service in red, tea service in grey and dinner service in shining bronze-black box. The dessert service is listed as containing 'rosy-cheeked apples, black grapes, oranges, melon, a bunch of bananas and a dish of mixed fruit'. In the breakfast box there were 'bread, poached eggs, ham, crescents, pork-pie, sausage'. The dinner set comprised 'chicken, fish, tart, cutlets, ham (with paper frill) and iced pudding'. There was, says the paper, 'no end to the fancy cakes, chocolate cakes, blancmanges, jellies, etc'.

The types of shop to be found – some manufactured, some made at home – include milliners, butchers, toy, haberdashers, sweet and confectionery, stationers, greengrocers, fish, flower, cooked meats/pies, newsagents, apothecaries/chemists, etc. The modern counterpart would be a toy garage with model cars and petrol pumps.

Schools
During the nineteenth century, the younger children of the middle and upper classes had

governess tuition in the privacy of their own homes, but the masses learned their basic academic skills at the local village school and left as soon as they could find employment and contribute to the meagre family budget.

Gradually, school education became more general and inevitably the toy-makers offered the model schoolroom. One suspects that the child owners enjoyed the opportunity to reverse roles – to command and punish misbehaving dolls and pay off old scores!

Like the model shops, it is the detail of the schoolroom which intrigues the collector; the tiny slates with sponges, the minute books and chalks and, above all, the set of identical little dolls who sat at desk or bench.

Bread and Circuses
Besides the utilities of life, the amusements of the time were copied as playthings. Schoenhut of America (see Note on page 27) manufactured and exported 'The Humpty

A chocolate shop in the elegant French style. The gold and grey painted interior, with shelves of tiny beribboned boxes, illustrates the days when buying presents of choice chocolates was a matter for leisurely shopping.

Late 19th century/French/Size: 22in wide x 20in high

Above
A school. Constructed as a box, this model is papered and painted to resemble a school building. The roof folds back and the front opens to reveal the classroom; the inside walls show coloured scenes and maps with 'progress and report' cards attached. Behind the schoolmistress can be seen blackboard, easel and abacus. The dolls have bisque heads, painted plaster legs with yellow shoes and are dressed in black dresses with lace collars. The teacher is a bisque doll with moulded hair, wearing a high-fastening cotton dress and black apron. On the outside of the roof, below the gable, the hands of the paper-faced clock point to three minutes to eight o'clock.

c 1900/French/Size: 17½ x 8 x 12in

Dumpty Circus Toy', a boxed set patented in 1907 which proved to be one of the outstanding toys of the turn of the century. Their sales booklet listed 34 accessories, 15 figures, 37 animals and illustrated an astonishing variety of circus figures – clowns, acrobats, heavyweight man, lady rider, ringmaster, liontamer, etc, and a menagerie of trained wild animals besides the domestic types of performing horse, donkey, pig, goat, etc.

Other manufacturers made cheaper circus toys of painted tin-plate. Collectors will find tumbling clowns, performing seals, trick cyclists, balancing figures and 'bucking' donkeys. The principal firms in this field were Martin of France and Lehmann of Germany.

Fairs were not always hoop-la and candyfloss. In the fifteenth century they were famous annual events attended by local folk, traders and foreign merchants. Through the centuries the serious business of buying and selling became intermixed with the simple enjoyment of a holiday and the chance to meet old friends.

It is the amusement factor which survived into the twentieth century and one of the greatest of the early showmen must surely have been Barnum, the famous American. In 1871, his 'Greatest Show on Earth' toured the world and 'Barnum & Bailey' became household names.

The toy-makers imitated all the fun of the fair: the mechanical music, swings, slides, helter-skelter, and the horses on the shining brass poles of the roundabout. Even today these toys are evocative of muddy fields, glittering prizes and unobtainable coconuts.

Circuses were one thing, bread was another and food was everyone's concern. Womenkind has always had to cook and kitchen toys are amongst the oldest and most delightful. Some were tiny copies of the real thing – small enough to fit into a dolls' house; others were scale models which could be used with fuel and made to work. It was the miniature size which appealed to children and which now attracts the collector; the gathering together of tiny pots and pans, dishes and utensils of every kind, so that the mind's eye already begins to prepare a dish and sees smoke curling from the polished stove. There were also rare specimen kitchens of gold and bronze for the nobility, but perhaps the strangest kitchen of all is illustrated in Flora Gill Jacobs' book *A History of Dolls' Houses*. It was a mid-nineteenth century doll with a kitchen contained within its opening skirt! The model kitchens of the last century remain unsurpassed for realism in toy-making.

Left
The Humpty Dumpty Circus Toy. The jointed figures, advertised as unbreakable, are made of solid wood, leather, and rubber and painted in enamel colours. They are so accurately constructed that they can balance in an endless variety of positions thus 'training eye and hand' and encouraging the 'gift of creation'.
The circus accessories included – circus tent, ring, tight-rope, ladder, chair, flexible cages, tubs, hoops, balancing rod, parasol, horizontal bar and so on. The parts could be purchased separately and used with other groups of the circus toy.
Size: The figures vary in size:
        Clown 7½in
        Large horse 6½in
        Chair 4½in
        Ladder 8½in

c 1907/American (The catalogue carries the inscription 'PAT U.S.A. Jan 29 1907')

Above
A three-sided model kitchen with everything handy for cooking and cleaning. Items include pestle and mortar, an oil lamp hanging on the wall, a sink with running water, a coffee grinder – all presided over by a uniformed servant. Everything was here for a small girl to play with and thereby to learn the first lessons in housewifery. The eighteenth century German kitchens of Nuremburg were the originals of this type of play-as-you-learn toy.

c 1910/German/Size: 19in high x 37in long

Note for Collectors. Schoenhut, established 1872, also manufactured 'everlasting and unbreakable dolls', dolls' houses, small xylophones and pianos, wooden toys for home assembly, target toys, railroad stations and rubber ball games.

Less durable materials were also used for toy animals, and in 1915 the New York Toy and Novelty Works of America advertised stuffed horses (and many other animals) made in muslin, flannel, bearskin and plush.

In the same year, the firm of W. H. Norman & Co of Leeds were producing dappled rocking-horses, tricycle-horses, pull-horses, swing-horses and stool-horses.

Up until 1914, when the crisis of World War I caused speedy development of motorised transport, the precedence of horse and carriage remained unchallenged. People and goods travelled the country relying on horses and ponies, waggons and carts. For centuries these were indispensable to everyday life and models of them were some of the earliest and most traditional toys.

The horses varied in size from the tiny examples, hand carved by the continental woodworkers of the 1700s, to the large rocking-horses of the nineteenth century, and were made from wood, wood covered in hide with flowing horsehair mane and tail, paper or card, cast metal, tin etc.

Toy carriages too came in all sorts of styles and sizes, from the rural cart to the horse 'bus and the smart equipage for town life. Stabling was not forgotten and complete toys were assembled with everything necessary for 'taking to the road'.

The variety of possible examples is evident when one considers that almost all the services requiring mobility were once horsedrawn: fire engines, stage coaches, ambulances, governess carts, omnibuses, gun carriages, removal and delivery vans, mail coaches etc. These, together with military chargers, fairground steeds, the performing circus horse and race games with dice all served as inspiration for the toy-makers who even produced a toy forge and blacksmith to effect repairs and restoration.

Noah's Ark

Noah's Ark was one of the most durable toys and has a history of at least two centuries. Made originally in the woodcarving areas of Germany, firstly as a cottage project and later as a guild industry, it was eventually mass-produced and has kept its form and character through the years. Part of its charm was the never-ending line of wild and domestic animals waiting for entry – and two of each! Some arks were furnished with over 300 pieces. In religious households where Sunday observance was strict, its Biblical associations made it one of the few toys allowed on the Sabbath.

The ark was sometimes carved to resemble the houses of the people who made it and it was thus frequently constructed and decorated in local style. Some arks had a dove perched on the top and the following cautionary verses pasted beneath the opening roof:

> God saw men's wicked ways
> And nipped them in the bud,
> He let it rain for forty days
> And drowned them with a flood.
> The bad all died, but mark!
> God saved good Noah's life.
> He saved him in a mighty Ark
> With his three sons and wife.
> And two of every kind
> Of insect, beast and bird –

> As He had said, for you will find
> God always keeps his word.
> So now with you and me
> Be this well understood –
> If bad, we too shall punished be,
> But blessed if we are good.

It is interesting to note that in the painted examples of the animals, the difference in colouration between the male and female of the species was correctly indicated. Scale was another matter, the butterfly being one quarter the size of the elephant and the grasshopper half as big as the monkey!

Note: An ark with its trail of animals looks most impressive if it can be displayed against a mirror background.

Soldiers

Miniature soldiers have been in existence since men fought each other and kings taught princes the art of war. Small carved figures are known from antiquity, examples in lead and bronze have survived from medieval times and model soldiers worked in silver were commissioned for European courts. Louis XIII was given 300 silver soldiers by his mother when he was a boy.

Although warriors made from costly metals were the playthings of the rich, toymakers quickly found cheaper materials and made replicas of wood, paper, celluloid, papier mâché and, later, metal alloys. The

A fine toy carriage with two horses on a wheeled platform. The sprung carriage has excellent detail with buttoned seats and opening doors. The horses are of painted plaster on wood with leather harness and horse-hair manes and tails. The little items of luggage are especially interesting – small trunks, hat-boxes etc.
Late 19th century/Scottish/Length with horses: 48in
The example illustrated must have been very costly, but there were painted tin horse and carriage toys made in Germany for the English market (about 1890) and these cost only one penny, so it would seem that almost every child could have a horse and cart.

Left
A carved and painted ark showing Noah, his family and a selection from sixty six pairs of animals, birds and insects, including butterflies and grasshoppers, which could all be packed neatly away inside.

Mid-19th century/German/Length: 17in

Below
Scissors toy. Twelve brightly painted wooden soldiers with bases pegged onto the trellis; thus as they are moved backwards and forwards they keep their orderly positions in advance and retreat. The set is packed in a wooden box with the curled wood shavings typical of the Victorian period.

c 1890/German for the English market/Length extended: 31in; soldiers 7½in

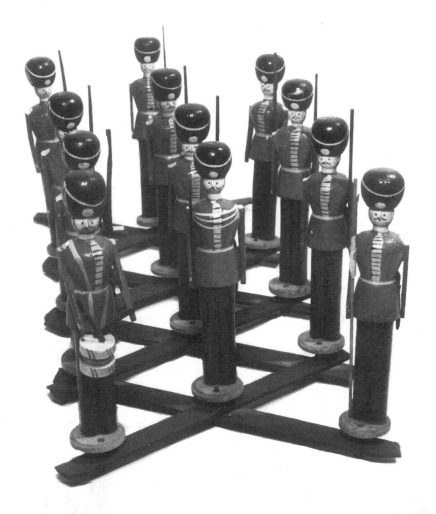

Above
A set of wooden military figures from the Erzgebirge carvers of Germany, a district famous for its production of bright little figures and wooden trees. The set consists of 67 soldiers, 67 tents, 33 trees and 6 cannon contained in an oval matchwood box. The making of these boxes, used for all sorts of toy wares, was a craft industry in itself. The painted and decorated examples are generally earlier than the plain variety.

First half of the 19th century/German/Size: soldiers 1⅞in

29

tinsmiths of Nuremburg produced small, flat metal figures known as 'German flats' and these were the forerunners of the lead 'solids' popular during the last quarter of the nineteenth century.

German supremacy in this section of the toy trade was challenged in the 1890s by William Britain, the British manufacturer whose firm eventually conquered the market with the 'hollow cast' soldier, sold in boxed sets. This was the toy soldier that dominated all domestic battles until plastic models eliminated forever the hazard of 'death by treading' on the nursery floor.

Besides the men and their personal weapons and armament, many other aspects of the military scene were modelled in authentic detail: tents, stockades, forts, standard-bearers, field hospitals, ambulances and so on. The attention to accuracy lavished on these little models enables the collector to trace not only the uniforms of nations, but also the development of their armies' fire power and transport.

Changes which help dating were the adoption of khaki battledress and steel helmets by the British army, of field grey by the Germans, and the formation of the Territorial Army just before World War I. Those were turbulent times and the wars of the British Empire and of foreign countries initiated new sets of models which can be dated accordingly.

Studying the items available the collector will realise that the toy-makers did not specialise in units of the British army; they also modelled knights in armour, cowboys, Indians etc. Some of the rarer models manufactured by the Britain firm were the non-military issues – the footballers of 1904, the boy scouts founded by Baden-Powell in 1908, and the Salvation Army figures.

Perhaps because it was easier to fight land battles on the table top than to simulate an encounter by sea, there have been many more toy soldiers than sailors or airmen. Nevertheless, all branches of the Services were represented in the toy field. Nor did manufacturers overlook ceremonial occasions as, for instance, the coronation coach and escort, bandsmen etc. Toy collectors, as distinct from model soldier collectors, should seek examples representing the developments in scale and the different materials used in manufacture.

Production of military models always increased in wartime and decreased afterwards when patriotic fervour diminished. Thus in the inter-war years, the same manufacturers produced peaceful country scenes and farm sets.

Large Horses

As nursery rhymes recall, the first rocking-horse was probably an obliging adult knee upon which a child could jog up and down; collectors however will have to begin with the hobby-horse. This was a medieval toy consisting of a carved horse's head topping a wooden stick or rod which trailed on the ground behind the rider who would stand astride the rod, grasping the reins or handles, and then imitate a galloping movement. What ultimately became training for grown-up duties started as imitative play, and children copied their elders who worked and rode horses as an essential part of daily life.

From the early hobby-horses developed the horse on rockers, carved from the solid and mounted on bentwood rockers. Furniture makers employed the same principle for rocking-chairs and cradles, but the horse ride could be more exciting – the greater the curve the more alarming the ride!

The cruder and usually older type of rocking-horse consisted of little more than a

Examples of Russian cavalry, infantry, and cannon from the Brocke collection of Heinrichsen Zinnfiguren. The figures are coloured in detail and are in excellent condition.

Early 19th century/German/Size: cavalry 1½in

Heinrichsen of Nuremburg was famous for the production of flat-cast military figures. Hilpert had preceded him, but it was Heinrichsen who is credited with standardisation (to a scale of 30mm) known thereafter as the 'Nuremberg' size.

Examples of hollow-cast military figures (top 3 rows) and historical figures (bottom row). Some of Britain's most saleable lines were models of the British Guards, mounted, foot and bandsmen. The first line in 1893 was of the Life Guards and, because numerous sets of Guardsmen were produced, collectors will find these more easily and cheaply than the rarer models, such as those connected with the Boer War, or the early gun teams and waggons. Details of dress and design can help to date a collection more accurately. For instance, oval bases and figures with fixed arms generally preceded those with movable arms.

First quarter of the 20th century/British/Size: bandsmen 2½in

Background (with rider): large dappled horse on swing bars. The fixed saddle has removable attachments for riding side-saddle if preferred. There are adjustable stirrups, and the mane and tail are of real horse-hair.

c 1950 (a traditional design used from about 1880)/English/Size: 47in on base x 43in long

Centre left: hide-covered horse on detachable platform – a dual purpose rocker and pull-toy, typical of Victorian times.
c 1890/English/Size: 30in high on rockers x 24in long

Centre right: an unusual horse on three iron-rimmed wheels, with wooden body painted dark brown, and metal head. It is chain driven and has decorated iron panels fixing the horse to the axle of the back wheels. (A somewhat similar design was still on sale in 1907). Horse tricycles were also made in England in the late nineteenth century, sometimes with two wheels in front and one at the back.

c 1860/American/Size: 29in high x 32in long

America possesses fine examples of early rocking-horses, often home-made. Amongst her immigrant population came craftsmen who brought with them the traditional skills of wood-carving from their European homelands.

Foreground: solid carved horse on curved rockers, with hand-holds on the arch of the neck. (A greater curve to the rockers usually denotes an earlier horse). Unpainted with replacement mane and tail.

c 1840/English/Size: 22in high on rockers x 33in long

velocipede horse on 'new' rockers - note handle to neck. Circa 1910.

carved head and seat fixed between two pieces of curving wood – rather like a circle of solid wood cut in half and with no true rockers. Inevitably, the Victorian delight in improvement and ornamentation resulted in the change to the hide-covered steed on wheels which, since it was mounted on detachable rockers, could also be used as a pull-along toy. Sometimes the horse body was mounted on three large wheels (as a tricycle), or was fixed to a four-wheeled plat-form with a handle at the rear for use as a push-along toy.

Towards the end of the nineteenth century and into Edwardian times, the true rocking-horse gave pride of place to the swing-bar type. As before, the model was large, made of wood, but now painted and varnished

rather than skin covered. The dappled grey was a favourite, with the flowing mane and tail and the flaring nostrils of the fairground horse, giving the impression of great speed and power. Sadly it no longer rocked, but swung to and fro by means of metal rods affixed to parallel bars either side of the horse and a central wooden stand beneath it.

The British, perhaps not as thorough as the Germans in the manufacture of tin toys nor as artistic as the French in the produc-tion of dolls, certainly made fine model horses. Some were made by estate carpenters, but most were produced com-mercially. The toy-producing areas manufactured rocking-horses, stool, pole and velocipede horses, whilst one enter-prising firm marketed white wood animals

with either rockers or wheels, and designed as elephants, swans or fish!

Its modern descendant is cheaper and bounces by means of metal springs, although this is not a new idea, since Mr Crandall patented much the same novelty in America in the 1860s! The present interest in Victoriana has revived the craft of carving wooden horses on the old pattern. Although expensive to buy, they remain toys which can be handed down to succeeding generations, thus ensuring that the rocking-horse will continue its history of over 300 years.

Note
Collectors refurbishing an old rocking-horse may find upholstery firms or stables able to help with hair for manes or tails.

Toys That Move

String, wheels, mercury, weights, wind, heat, balance, torsion, springs, ratchet, trellis, sand, magnetism, electricity, steam and clockwork.

Wind, water and heat have long been used for motivation. One thinks of kites, the water toys of ancient civilisations and the 'angel chimes' of today which revolve when the candle is lit, and our fragile 'mobiles' of card and straw which hang suspended on a fine thread and are moved by circulating air or by warm air rising. In the same way the old toys which hung above the kitchen stove were motivated.

Air pressure was used in other ways to activate toys, sometimes by squeezing a rubber bulb connected to a tube so that the air moved the toy at the other end. (This was frequently used for joke toys – when plates were mysteriously moved by the operator seated at the other side of the table with the tube lying unnoticed beneath the cloth!) It was also used for such games as 'puff' billiards and in various swinging toys. Mercury combined with gravity motivated acrobatic toys – and the basic method of tilting the track enabled one of the first toy trains to edge safely down to ground level.

Wheels and springs, weights and string, balance and tension all played their part in making toys move. It will be interesting for the collector to seek examples showing the greatest range of motivation methods. Given here is a sample list from a wide selection:

Hand	Push-up on stick, hoops, bouncing and swinging toys, floor or carpet toys.
String	Tops, 'pantins'.
Wheels	Pull-toys.
Mercury	Acrobatic toys.
Weights	Pecking hens, women washing, knitting etc.
Wind	Kites, 'sail' toys, whistles (breath toys), squeeze-boxes, bellows toys.
Heat	Steam, chime and revolving toys.
Clockwork	Transport, tin-plate toys and automata.
Balance	Tumbling and performing toys.
Torsion	Lever and cable toys.
Springs	Jack-in-the-boxes, surprise toys.
Ratchet	Found in metal animal and transport toys.
Scissors (trellis)	Wooden soldiers, and other peasant-type toys.
Sand	Leotard, juggler etc.
Magnetism	Fishing game.
Electricity	Electric trains.

The simplest way of moving an object is to pull or push it along, and for centuries before Victorian times pull-toys had been fashioned by peasant societies. It was, however, the excellent work of the wood-carvers of Germany which finally spread beyond local frontiers and into foreign markets. Strong, simple and brightly painted examples of their carved and turned toys filled the pedlars' packs, the merchants' stores and, eventually, the children's nurseries in many parts of the world.

The Victorian pull-toys were more sophisticated – usually mounted on wooden platforms and with totally inadequate metal wheels. Beneath the wooden platform was an arrangement of metal rods connected to the axle of the wheels and to the figures on top of the platform. The movement of the wheels altered the position of the rods and caused the heads or limbs of the figures to move in a simple pattern. Thus, an arrangement upon the platform became a performing group whilst the toy was in motion. They were often amusing – cockerels which could crow, cows which could moo and give milk by means of a fillable compartment at the back! Horses, clowns, musicians, animals with performing riders, and so on – they lined the shelves of Victorian toyshops and, being strong and well made, they are still available and reasonably priced for today's collector.

Sand toys Falling sand was one of the most ingenious ways of effecting movement. Sand toys worked on the principle of a succession of small buckets or 'hoppers' fastened to a wheel, with a reservoir of sand above – somewhat like a funnel. A small hole at the tapering end enabled the sand to trickle through, fill the 'hoppers' and thus turn the wheel to which was affixed an axle with a light cut-out figure fastened to it. To set the figure in motion, the box containing the wheel would have to be turned two or three times and always to the right. The movement was quite long lasting and the figure, with loosely fastened limbs, achieved all sorts of

Above

The larger figure is an unusual 'bellows' toy. The velvet-covered squeeze box contains the bellows movement which produces musical notes when depressed. The doll has a bisque head and wooden limbs with movable arms; it is affixed to the platform, and is moved by means of the differing pressures applied to the drum. Dressed as a jester in lace-trimmed silks, with bells on cap, hands and swinging rope.

Victorian/German head/Height on box: 26in

The two bisque-headed musicians are mounted on a platform and play cymbals and hand-bells as the toy is pushed or pulled along. Connecting rods attached to the wheel shafts activate the figures – the front wheels move the hind figure and the back wheels move the front figure. Dressed in blue and red with gold trim.

Victorian/German dolls/Height on box: 12½in

Right

Heat toy of a lighthouse. A metal cap at the top of the tower held a small candle; when lit, the heat caused the vanes to turn the circle of coloured lights.

c 1900/English/Height: 6½in

Above

Wooden train and track. Trevithick's locomotive *Catch Me Who Can* and Stephenson's *Rocket* were part of early railway history. It is amazing, therefore, that there should be a toy train in existence only some fifteen years later, when railways had not yet become a part of ordinary life. To a collector this must surely be the start of a truly representative collection of toy trains. The design of the train itself was enchanting: a wooden puff of 'smoke' streamed out behind the engine, and the carriages, with open windows and minute passengers inside, were gaily decorated with flower motifs; even the solid wooden wheels were patterned. The track looked like a grooved ruler and was made of wood (real railways did not have successful metal track until about 1838); the toy model had to be pushed along the straight and up the incline until it reached the highest point, when it slid gently down again.

c 1845/1850/German/Sizes: engine 4½in long; carriages 2½in long

Below the wooden train is a tin-plate 'carpet' or pull-along toy, with engine, tender and ten carriages. Painted in gay colours with flimsy spoke wheels and the tab-and-slot method of assembly.

c 1860/70/German/Size: engine and carriages 2¾in long

33

acrobatic and eccentric postures and actions.

Stick toys These toys consisted of two sticks with a loosely joined figure fastened to the top of each. As the hollow end of one stick slid to and fro upon the other, the little object was pushed along, up, over and then back again. Usually, animals were represented, the monkey being the most common in England. The carving was sometimes crude, but its prototype was cheap and popular throughout Europe.

Torsion The force of twisted string was responsible for motivating many toys. As in so many examples of uncomplicated toys with movement, it was really the free-moving limbs which gave the little figures such gaiety and charm as they swung from their twisted string between supporting posts.

Swinging weights This simple method of effecting movement has been used in most European countries, notably in those with special skills in woodcarving. It is still reproduced today. Like so many folk toys, different countries made various arrangements of animals, birds and domestic scenes, but all used the same principle. An obvious example is that of the 'pecking hens', their beaks pecking and their tails flicking as the weighted string swung and rotated below the platform to which they were fixed. There were also models of a

Above
The acrobat at right is wood and composition with painted moustache and imperial. The loosely jointed figure packed into the drawer in the box base and the reversed lid became part of the steps.

c 1860/German/Size: acrobat 4½in; box 6½in long

At left is another wooden acrobat with metal weighted head and loose leg-joints, who somersaults realistically and even stands on his head.

Mid-19th century/German/Size: 7in

Above
A painted tin-plate cat with ratchet start. The cat appears to have two tails because the metal ratchet is slotted above the tail and motivates the heavy flywheel beneath the cat.

c 1890/German/Length: 9in

Scissors toy of peasant couples, gaily coloured in yellow, blue, pink and green.

Mid-20th century by Yootha Rose/Length extended: 14in

Skipping couple. A thin metal rod passes through the hands of both children and lifts the girl doll by means of a cam within the body. The metal skipping 'rope' works off the same shaft and therefore keeps perfect time with the lifting of the body. The dolls have bisque heads, the hair is real and they are dressed in period clothes.

Late 19th century/English/Height: 5in

Right
At left is a sand toy of 'Leotard'. Contained in a glazed box, the flimsy card acrobat was affixed to a spindle and performed innumerable tricks on his trapeze. Because he was fully jointed, with free-moving limbs, the trickling sand at the back enabled him to execute unexpected and intricate movements. A fair number of different sand toys were available – Leotard, jigging minstrel, monkeys, organ-grinder etc. All were accompanied by the strict instruction 'To be turned twice to the right'.

c 1870/1880/Size: box 8in x 9¼in; figure 3¼in

At right is a comic torsion toy of painted wood. The pressure on the one movable support and the tension of the twisted string through the fully jointed figure enabled the toy to be manipulated so that it performed all sorts of tricks and somersaults; it could even be stopped in mid-air.

Early 20th century/American/Height: 17in

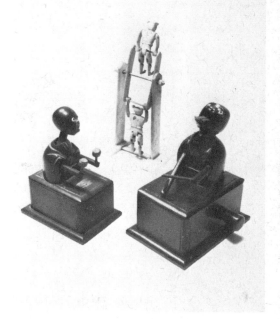

woman churning, performing animals, musicians, etc.

Spring toys Probably the best known spring toy is the Jack-in-the-box. When the lid was removed, the release of the compressed spring ejected a face or figure at an alarming speed, causing more shock than surprise. Similarly, the spring recoil action was used to shoot pellets with devastating inaccuracy from innumerable toy guns.

Springs were also used for moderate movement and, combined with balance, they could give a lengthy performance, as in the American 'Slinky', which was a coiled but not compressed spring that descended the stairs end over end when pushed gently over the first step. Minute springs also moved the little robins that decorated Christmas trees and cakes.

Scissors toy This used an old idea, applied not only to toys but also to the design for invalids' 'lazy tongs'. The wooden figures were pegged to the open frame of crossed laths and moved backwards and forwards as the trellis was opened and closed. It was a folk toy, decorated with many different motifs.

String motivated toys Tops of many kinds were – and are – amongst the world's best loved toys. They have spun and hummed their way through the centuries and there were hundreds of different models, shapes and sizes. Besides the more usual form, the same method was used to give movement to little spinning figures.

Simple movements were also possible when the string was attached to freely moving limbs as in the 'Pantins', or Dancing Jack puppets. It has survived more rarely as a very simple way of automation, when the string passing through the body of the figure moved head or limbs when pulled from below.

There can be no strict chronological order for dating moving toys, since folk toys with movement continued to be made long before and after the coming of steam, clockwork and electricity.

Balance toys The movement of balance toys was sometimes minimal, as in the nodding figures which simply moved their heads when tilted. They were poised so as to preserve equilibrium, and would swing gently, then return to their original positions when momentum ceased. Balance, combined with weights and the force of gravity, was a method of moving simple toys known throughout the world and the same idea is still used today in folk toys from many lands, and in souvenir toys from Africa.

In this category came the 'topple' toys (there were many variations of these little self-righting figures – usually clowns or animals) and the performing acrobat. The clown type had a weighted base and the acrobat contained free mercury which altered position and enabled him to somersault backwards down three steps.

Magnetic toys Although pocket magnets have been a boy's delight for many years, magnetic toys were not made in great variety. The best known is probably the 'fishing' game, when a small magnet attached to a rod caught a fish with a metal ring through its head. (The rod was also useful for picking up mother's sewing pins!) Another popular toy of the 1880s was a boxed set of fishes and ducks which were moved over a basin of water by a magnet.

Electricity Collectors may think that electrical toys are modern, but this is not the case. In the 1880s the following battery-operated toys were advertised – electric railway, electric screwboat, electric swing with model figures etc. Only a few years later other transport toys were made and, as electricity became fully available, they were followed by the electric train sets which have developed in sophistication and popularity until the present day. In America, perhaps the best known manufacturers of electrical toys were Garlick, Ives and Lionel, and European collectors should seek examples of their products.

Some toys with movement were almost too fragile to survive – the early 'planes which were wound up with a rubber band, the feathered bird which fluttered down a stick, the tiny man who danced in a liquid-filled tube and so on. With such a wide range of movements to study, the field for the collector is varied and unusual; the items

mentioned in this brief survey may be doubled as he discovers the many ingenious ways in which toys were made to move.

Steam

Steam for powering wagons, tractors, rollers and so on replaced the horse for hauling heavy loads. The heyday of steam ended when the lorry took over heavy haulage on the roads and the diesel superseded the steam engine. Steam toys were a boy's delight, engendering exciting smells, noise and the prospect of disaster. The toy steam engine, fuelled with methylated spirits, provided the driving power for many working models. To any mechanically minded youngster this was a new dimension – power and movement were suddenly and dramatically available.

The early English single-cylinder vertical toy steam engine was cheaply produced and soon rivalled by the products of the German firms of Bing and Marklin. A correspondent reporting in the trade paper *The British Toymaker* of November 1916 wrote: 'The toy industry developed by Germany was divided into two parts. There were, in the first place, the metal goods for which extensive and valuable machinery was used. Whilst Birmingham twenty or thirty years ago was making the small steam locomotive with the old-fashioned type of boiler, like a tin can, and a piece of tube at the top to represent the chimney, the Germans set their minds to the problem of producing an exact copy in miniature of the London and North Western and the London and South Western Railway engines. Seeing that the old-fashioned type of engine was the best that Birmingham could then do, the trade left England and went to Germany.'

Steam had really caught the imagination by the end of the nineteenth century and a good range of stationary steam engines, steamships and locomotives was available in the toyshops. These will not be too difficult for today's collector to find. The early toy steam road-vehicles, however, were produced in fewer numbers and consequently are scarce today. They date to the early years of the twentieth century and the manufacturers were chiefly German or French. The novelty steam items are perhaps

Above
Two string motivated toys. At left is a toy with action similar to the spinning top. The string is wound round the pillar beneath the platform and the figure is attached by means of a metal rod. When the string is pulled, the momentum produced causes the figure to whirl round at speed whilst the loosely jointed legs swing freely. The doll is wooden with a parian head and is dressed in a royal-blue suit.

c 1896 (named and dated box)/French/Height: 10in including metal base

At right is a composition and wood toy of an old lady darning. The string passes through the body and when pulled activates the head and right arm to imitate the action of darning the stocking held in the left hand. The spectacles are of brass with glass 'lenses' and the toy is named and dated on the base.

c 1817/German/Height: 8in

Above
Tremble toys. These three iron cats have movable heads, fixed inside the body by a thin steel strip. They nod when touched.

Late 19th century/English/Height: 3in

Above
A woman churning whilst her cat laps milk; a swinging-weight toy of carved and painted wood, sometimes called a pendulum toy. Strings connected the moving parts of the toy with the weight beneath.

Early 20th century/European, probably German/Height: 4¾in

Above
At top, a skipping toy of painted tin, with china doll; the movement is produced by spring, wheel and string. The large wheel is moved by a spring with string attached and the doll turns accordingly. The shaft is connected to the wheel and goes through the doll's shoulders.

Early 20th century/English/Height: 6¼in

Bottom left, Jack-in-the-loaf, a small joke toy made of wood and compressed cardboard. A catch at the base releases a spring which pops out of the loaf pushing off the top crust. The spring is topped by a small head wearing a monocle.

Mid-20th century/English/Height: 4in

At right, pig-on-a-stick. The roughly carved pig is pushed along the stick, goes over the top and is returned to the base of the stick by pulling down the wooden slide.

Victorian folk toy/Length extended: 11½in

Left
At left a balance toy, typical of many simple toys found all over the world (carved wood in Africa, brass in India etc). The central figure supports a curved and weighted balancing aid. The shoulders are jointed and wherever he stands, and at almost any angle, he will not topple or fall. Wooden Dutch-type doll on modern stand.

Mid-19th century/English/Size: doll 4in

At right a 'nodding' figure of composition and plaster. The head rests on horizontal metal supports at the neck and is free-moving, so that it nods as the figure is tilted. Similar action is found in ornamental china figures, as well as in toys, and very often the toy figures wear metal spectacles and are seated in rustic chairs.

c 1880/German (often made in pairs of man and woman)/Height seated: 6in

the rarest. What collector would not delight to find 'the smallest steamboat in the world, the Minotaur Petite of only 2ins and warranted to work by steam round a basin of water', the steam fire engine which really pumped water, or the Dancing Nigger which danced by steam for one hour at each operation? All were on sale in England in 1884.

In the adult world, steam began to oust sail in the early nineteenth century, but it was not until the late eighteen hundreds that steam ships began to be popularly available as toys. Radiquet of France made some fine models and it is true to say that the German and French manufacturers led the industry in this respect.

A rare catalogue of 1884 illustrates and describes a variety of steam toys – vertical, horizontal and beam engines, fire engines, locomotives, boats and paddle steamers, priced from one shilling to two pounds. Even the cheapest had brass components, whilst the Express locomotive had brass boiler and framework, copper back, eight brass flanged wheels, safety valve, bell, whistle, water-tap, starting lever, name-plate and furnace and could run 'backwards or forwards'!

One of the most satisfying uses for the stationary steam engine was with Meccano models (see Indoor Games, Constructional Toys and Pastimes). In 1915 the Meccano steam engine (probably made by an outside manufacturer for Meccano) was described as having a 'highly finished vertical boiler made of oxidised brass, with stationary cylinder, eccentric reverse-gear, water gauge, spring safety-valve, etc.' The fittings were nickelled and the boiler fixed on a cast base.

There were other English makers of good quality engines. The Norfolk firm of Bowman Jenkins advertised steam engines which could drive twenty or more models and the largest Meccano model. Steam, of course, could be dangerous and one of the great selling points of the Bowman steam toys was the use of the new safety valve, making good their claim 'Steam for all with absolute safety'. The Midland firm of Malins (Engineers) Ltd, founded in 1935, made the popular Mamod models and, happily, is still doing so.

Above

A vertical, single-cylinder steam engine of sturdy construction. It has a copper boiler, brass chimney and cast-iron, drilled base plate. Trademark GBN for the firm of Bing. The trademark later changed to the capital letters BW, the B inverted over the W.

c 1910/German/Height: 12½in

In the foreground are four tin-plate craftsmen with their belt-driven tools of grinding wheel, stamping press, wood saw and metal saw. The base plates are drilled for securing to stands.

c 1910/German/Height: figures 4in; base plates 4½ x 2½in and 5 x 2¾in

Right

Two brass and steel Bowman driving engines with the original box showing trademark of Indian with bow and arrow. The low gear drive was designed to take Meccano-size pulley wheels and the metal base plates were drilled with standard Meccano pattern equidistant holes. This arrangement between the two firms brought realism to the young engineer, enabling him to drive his models under authentic working conditions.

c 1927-1933/English/Size: height with chimney 6½in; base 5½ x 5½in

Above

A steam locomotive by Carette, a Frenchman working in Nuremberg from the end of the nineteenth century until World War I. Many of his products were imported for sale in England and there were differently designed trademarks. This engine carries the entwined initials GC for Georges Carette & Cie.

Early 20th century/German for the English market/Length: 8½in

The company also produced model railway accessories – signalling equipment, lighting, station buildings, tunnels, bridges etc and other metal toys including steamships and marine figures.

Above

A green and black Bowman steam locomotive model 4-4-0, mounted on original track with wooden sleepers and metal ties. A long, low express type with good scale appearance, 'brass and steel throughout'. This firm also made a smaller model, the 0-4-0, with complementary rolling stock and four steam launches. Its toys were strong and would not catch fire when overturned.

c 1930/English/Size: length 12in; height 5in

Above
Two working models of different quality and materials for use with stationary steam engines. The gaily painted windmill is more fanciful than robust, whilst the churn is of heavy cast metal with glass container and is firmly screwed to the wooden base.

Early 20th century/German (GBN for Bing)/Height: windmill 8in, churn 9in

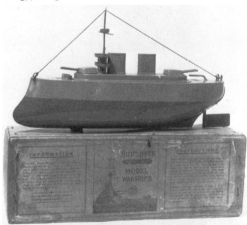

Above
A model steam warship in grey and red, fitted with copper flash boiler. The manufacturer claimed that 'one charge of spirit will drive the boat at a nice speed for one-and-a-half hours'. The box is the original. Made by J. W. Sutcliffe, Horsforth, Leeds, a firm manufacturing toys from about 1890-1920.

English/Size: 13in long x 5in high

For most toy collectors the word 'steam' conjures up a picture of a hissing locomotive, impatient, powerful and even dangerous. One thinks particularly of the English firm of Bassett-Lowke, the German firms of Bing, Carette and Marklin and the American firms of Beggs and Weeden. Early American model railway engines often carried a cow-catcher, bell and light – just as the originals would have done – to give warning of the train's approach along the miles of open track. The scale models of Bassett-Lowke, superb in workmanship and design, were but one end of a complete range. The firm made – and also had made for them in Germany – some of the finest steam trains, authentic toys which were the pride and joy of their owners, and which are now collectors' pieces in their own right. Goods and passenger trains, various engine classes, and the distinctive regional livery were all faithfully reproduced. These toy replicas of the real thing preserve, in miniature, some of the great names in railway history.

Many manufacturers of tin toys made working models for steam engines and often they were neither to scale, nor truly practical – who would really design a *windmill* powered by *steam*? J. Falk of Nuremberg, a maker of fine mechanical toys including moving picture machines and magic lanterns, also produced model steam engines and a great variety of working models to complement them. There were the usual tools – saws, hammers, grinding wheels (some accompanied by little tin figures assembled by the slot-and-tab method), windmills, swings, waterwheels, pumps, fountains, cranes, lighthouses, roundabouts and various other pieces of imaginative and totally unlikely apparatus! Fleischmann, Bing and numerous other factories produced these little working models, but as many of them were unmarked, it is often impossible to decide their origin, unless one is lucky enough to possess the original box.

Note for collectors
A steam passenger-carrying locomotive is a 'must' and whereas a scale model would be expensive, it will be possible to find an example of a toy steam engine. For display purposes, a complete layout will probably take up too much room, but an engine looks realistic mounted on a section of rail. A vertical stationary steam engine should be included, since these were the life-force of so many working models; many other toys powered by steam were advertised during the first half of the twentieth century, including motor cars.

There is now a growing interest in the age of steam and collectors will find steam models and toys increasingly sought after; nevertheless, they are well worth the search and the minor repairs so often necessary.

Clockwork
The logical progression from static models was to moving toys and man used his ingenuity to make them life-like in scale and performance.

At first, the hand-made examples were too expensive for the general public and most were exhibited by individual owners, or shown at entertainment halls as money-making concerns. Delighted crowds gathered to watch the performances and those with accompanying music were an even greater attraction. In 1851 Mayhew interviewed and wrote of an Italian exhibitor whose stock-in-trade included little figures who moved their eyes and limbs, a carriage with galloping horses, a dancing Tyrolese peasant (wound up under her petticoats) and a lady with plate in hand who received money from the audience! His most prized exhibit, however, and the children's greatest favourite, was a mechanical elephant with rolling eyes, curling trunk and moving tail. Mounted on the elephant was a little Indian driver who took aim with bow and arrow. The Italian exhibitor imported his figures from Paris and Germany and mentioned that the musical boxes were made in Geneva. All these delights and many others he showed in the streets and in the *palais de gin* and public houses. Many of these more elaborate clockwork toys are dealt with under the section 'Automata'.

Clockwork and the principle of expanding springs revolutionised the toy world. No longer were toys merely pushed or pulled, their delighted owners could now wind them up and watch the marvel of independent movement. As machinery replaced handwork, clockwork mechanisms were no longer costly and mass production brought cheap clockwork toys within the range of most manufacturers and into ordinary homes.

Inexpensive metal alloys were light, and could be pressed out in hundreds and fitted with clockwork mechanisms. The cheap tinplate examples were many and varied. Some clockwork tin toys incorporated mechanical music and there were musical boxes especially made for children. The models were round or square and the price varied according to the number of tongues. Besides these little boxes with their tinkle tunes, children also enjoyed musical chairs (which played up to three airs when sat upon), cuckoo clocks and musical photograph albums.

It is easy to appreciate the vast field available. Clockwork could motivate dolls (those with light, hollow bodies – see 'Mechanical Dolls'), engines, cars, boats and novelties of all kinds. Simple adjustments to wheels and cams could produce amusing and eccentric variations of speed and direction.

Trains deserve a special mention. Clockwork immediately brings to mind a passenger or goods train circling the floor, preferably with model station and signalling equipment to complete the realism. However inventive clockwork tin toy manufacturers became, it is the train sets for which they are principally remembered.

No account of clockwork trains, however brief, would be complete without a tribute being paid to the genius of Frank Hornby, founder of Meccano Ltd, whose early constructional toy was followed by Hornby trains, Dinky toys and the Hornby-Dublo system.

Hornby also made many railroad accessories – the turntables, points, water tanks, buffers and signal and station equipment, so that the railway scene could be built up, changed at will, and additions given as presents. In some families an old table, landing, or attic would be given over to the 'trains', but once the lay-out had been permanently set out, the fun of putting it all together had often disappeared. Landscape items could also be purchased and the excitement of seeing the train emerge from the tunnel or pick up the mail sack as it sped past, were thrills that never entirely

vanished. The firm, which started in a single room where the first sets were packed, developed into a factory of world renown.

In England, the firm of Bassett-Lowke was, and still is, famous for its model and toy locomotives. Many of their earlier productions were made by the German firm of Bing for Bassett-Lowke, and some in co-operation with Marklin. Marklin also had a good trade in station accessories – track, bridges and signalling equipment, often of hand-painted tin-plate until World War I, and later lithographed.

The German exporters, two of the best known being Bing and Marklin, worked for the English and American markets, the items bearing the specific decoration of the importing countries. By contrast, fewer American firms exported to Europe, hence examples from their factories are more difficult for an English collector to acquire.

In addition to many other metal toys, the firm of Bing made a variety of road vehicles, the early enamelled examples – as distinct from the lithographed tin types – being rare and thus valuable collectors' pieces. They had fine accessories – lamps, working handbrakes and white solid rubber tyres. The BW trademark indicates that the model was made after 1919.

E. P. Lehmann of Brandenburg, originally a metal box maker, turned to toy-making in the late nineteenth century and continued to make lithographed tin-plate toys through the early part of the twentieth century and up until World War I. They were marketed in Europe, America and Asia. Production continued after the war and the firm's miniature GNOM toys (with and without clockwork) date to the mid-1930s.

The toy collector, whatever rarities he may acquire, is most likely to come across tin toys by Lehmann or Bing (Germany) or Martin (France). These German firms also manufactured steam engines.

The coming of the motor car at the end of the nineteenth century gave the cheap toy-makers a huge field for expansion and, by the beginning of the twentieth century, both Germany and France were making and exporting them in vast numbers.

Similarly, the later development of the aeroplane was to inspire the toy-makers of

Above
Three tinplate toys by Fernand Martin, who manufactured tin toys from about 1880 until World War I. The figures, usually about 8-9in high, wore cheap clothing to disguise the mechanism and weighted feet. The initials F.M. are often found on top of the metal hats of the standing figures, as here.
Centre, *l'éminent avocat* standing in his box, moving head and body and gesticulating with both arms as if addressing the court.

Early 20th century/French/Height: 9in

At right, the violinist; a typical Martin toy, with movement in the 'bowing' arm.

c 1900/French/Height: 8in

At left, the drinker; similar in style to the violinist, with movement in head and both arms as he raises the glass to his lips.

Height: 8in

Above
Clockwork model of an early horseless carriage. It has lamps, driving column, wire wheels and wicker basket at the back. The collapsible fringed hood is of yellow cotton and the seat is now padded, but was originally silk-lined.

c 1895-1900/French/Size: 10½in long x 10½in high

Above
Two Bing clockwork cars of different quality
The larger is marked BW for Bing Werke and
has opening passenger doors. The attachment
moves the front wheels from left to right so the
car can change direction as it moves. A tin
chauffeur sits in the driving seat and the car is
finely decorated and in excellent condition.

Colours: Green/black/silvered radiator/Length:
11½in
The smaller car is also marked BW for Bing, but
would have been much cheaper. The detail is
only indicated and the car is assembled by the
tab-and-slot method.

Colours: Grey/black/Length: 5¼in

Above
Facing left, a model 4-4-0 clockwork locomotive
(Duke class) with the name of Bassett-Lowke on
the tender. Gauge O. Facing right, a clockwork
0-4-0 tank engine by Hornby. The livery is that
of the London, Midland and Scottish line and
the track is the tubular metal variety sold with
the train sets. Gauge O.

Above
The acrobat, with vigorous clockwork
movement. He somersaults by means of a strong
metal bar through the shoulders. Jointed at
thighs and shoulders, with porcelain head and
painted features.

c 1880/American (The American Mechanical
Toy Company)/Height on stand: 7½in

Above
Top, a metal rider on tricycle with fixed
direction. The metal face is painted and the
handle-bars go through the hands.

c 1880/Height of figure mounted: 10in

Bottom, a trick cyclist; the eccentric movement
enables the model to turn corners and perform
realistically. The rider has a fine painted
porcelain head and wooden hands.

c 1870/French/Height of figure mounted: 10½in

Note: American books and catalogues often
refer to this type of toy as a 'velocipede', of
which the bicycle and tricycle were
developments.

Above
Mechanical jigging figures. Foreground, two
plantation dancers with jointed wooden bodies,
each tap-dancing by means of a wire from the
wooden base.
Background, two skeletons operated in the same
manner.

c 1890/American (Ives)/Height: dancers 6in;
skeletons 11½in

Ives toys were so popular that the designs were
'pirated' and reproduced in Europe.

the post-war years. Clockwork aeroplanes were made, but very few were able to fly. Nevertheless, to a generation aware of flying machines, they looked realistic even if they only ran along a makeshift runway. World War I popularised the idea of air-borne toys – particularly the Zeppelin and the bi-plane, but as in the clockwork swing-boats and roundabouts, they were really anchored to the central support which revolved.

During World War I, imports from Germany and France came to an end and many British and American firms increased their manufacture of this type of toy. Birmingham had long been noted for its metal work, Liverpool and London for toy production. Early twentieth century manufacturers of mechanical and metal toys in England included Bedington, Liddiatt & Co Ltd, of Birmingham (also importers); Whiteley, Tansley & Co Ltd of Liverpool; Bings Ltd of London; British Lion Manufacturing Co of Letchworth, Herts; British Metal & Toy Manufacturers Ltd (BRIMTOY) of London; Star Manufacturing Co (Swan Toys) of London; G. & J. Lines, Ltd of London.

It is probably true to say that the collector of the future, seeking for our present-day clockwork toys as antiques, will find the majority were made in Japan or Hong Kong.

For the collector wishing to specialise, clockwork tin toys offer enormous scope. Some were purely imitative, such as trains and ships, but many were amusing, odd, even macabre. In 1884 one could buy for a few pence or shillings mechanical crocodiles, birds, zoo animals, beetles, walking and swimming ladies, omnibuses and water-carts, trick cyclists, jumping frogs, gesticulating lawyers, dancing negroes and skeletons! Steadily the market expanded and more oddities, novelties and ingenious items of all kinds were sold very cheaply and in great numbers. As with all true toys, the cheaper they were originally, the less likely they were to survive and the rarer they will be today. Do not despair of condition – a good penetrating oil works wonders for rusty springs, but it is advisable not to repaint.

Appreciation of the many fine American toys is a study in itself, but the names of George Brown (for mechanical and bell toys), and Ives and Lionel (for clockwork trains and other novelties) are three of the most famous in this specialised field.

The appeal of the nineteenth century tin toys is perhaps nowhere more apparent than in the wonderful range produced by George W. Brown & Company of America (founded in 1856 and later amalgamated with J. & E. Stevens). Many of his designs were completely original and he specialised in clockwork and mechanical devices, most of the horse-drawn transport items having the spoke wheels typical of the period and distinguished by their bright colours and sometimes fanciful metal decoration.

Let no collector imagine that tin toys, although made of a common material, are cheap. They have now reached sale-room prices quite disproportionate to their apparent worth, and prices for metal toys of the post World War II era are steadily increasing.

Note
The sturdy iron toys of the American manufacturers are unusual additions for the European collector, since iron was not a material generally used by the French or German toy industries.

A group of Lehmann tin toys. Top row, the stubborn donkey; the donkey bucks and the clown tries to control him. Adam the porter; a walking figure with hand-cart on two wheels. The mandarin, who travels in the sedan carried by two coolies (he can pull the pig-tail of the nearest coolie to make him hurry). Bottom row, the Zulu, the African post-cart with ostrich; the driver moves the reins whilst the ostrich nods its head as it walks. The crawling beetle, which crawls and opens and shuts its wings whilst moving. The performing sea-lion, with movable flippers.

Early 20th century/German

At left, mechanical ball-player; the painted figure whirls the balls at a furious rate whilst bending from side to side at the waist.

c 1910/Height: 8½in

At right, the painted tin figure of a policeman has moving legs and flapping arms.

Height: 9½in

Both are examples of the least expensive type of clever moving toy.

Centre, the waltzers; an ingenious pressed tin-plate toy which enables the dancers to waltz in circles. She is mounted on wheels beneath the skirt; he has one wheel beneath the left foot.

c 1900/German/Height: 8in

Busy Lizzie – the mechanical sweeper; the clockwork mechanism moves her forward, pushing her sweeper. Both arms move and the handle of the sweeper slides through the left palm.

Early 1900s/German/Height: 7in

A painted tin mechanical Scots piper; the clockwork movement in the base moves the arms as if he were playing the pipes and also activates the tinkle tunes.

c 1910/Height: 11in

The ostrich; a heavy metal toy with an unusual action in that the clockwork movement moves only the back leg, but so forcefully that it knocks against the foreleg and pushes the bird forwards. The neck swings freely.

Early 1900s/Height: 8½in

Automata

Automata have an ancient history, certainly religious in origin. Articulated figures with hollow bodies or heads have been discovered which could perform seemingly miraculous movements thanks to the operator hidden within who manipulated the strings. In primitive societies these visible signs of life from gods and goddesses must have been awe-inspiring. Likewise, the ceremonial masks used by early cultures in America, Europe and the East could be made to move – jaws, ears, eyes etc, and these too must be counted as the ancestors of automata.

Specifically, automaton means 'self-moving: a mechanical device which acts of itself: a piece of mechanism with concealed motive power'. Thus, primitive examples had to be motivated by simple devices – strings, rods and so on worked by human hands. Although such secret practices were impressive, mechanism as we understand it was completely undeveloped and centuries were to pass before man's ingenuity contrived the elaborate automata of today.

One of the most celebrated automata of all time was Vaucanson's famous duck, exhibited in France in 1738, which performed many functions of a live bird, including the digestive process! Throughout the ensuing years the best automata were of French, German or Swiss origin, the latter pre-eminent in the making of singing birds. London, too, had experts in this most specialised field. However, these lavish specimens, produced by skilled craftsmen of the eighteenth century, were at no time abundant. They were hand made, expensive and time-consuming to construct. Indeed, the secret of their invention was often zealously guarded.

Whilst these bejewelled and intricate novelties could be considered as playthings for adults, they were never intended as toys for children. The singing bird hidden in a tiny golden box, the life-size performing figure and the wonderful clocks with striking 'jacks' are not likely to be available for the buyer today. Nevertheless, the influence of these superior pieces persisted and some excellent automata were manufactured in the nineteenth century, frequently fitted with mechanical music.

Thus, the collector is still able to find desirable items, although the complicated ones with several movements and musical box will be more expensive. It is therefore better to seek simpler types of automated figures, animals, etc, and to include examples of the Victorian and Edwardian eras. The available range depends on one's pocket, but the little tin waltzing partners can be as fascinating as the 'breathing' lady or the performing monkey.

More specialists made automata than one at first supposes. The few early makers were perfectionists, but throughout the late eighteenth, the nineteenth and on into the twentieth century there were craftsmen working in Europe and London who specialised in specific aspects of automata – drinkers, smokers, magicians, conjurors, musicians etc. Smokers have always been popular: 'The Masher King', a smoking automaton figure advertised in 1884, was then priced at £6 6s 0d. Both smokers and tea-drinkers were then recommended to tobacconists and grocers for window displays. Many of these larger automaton figures were the products of the Vichy factory of Paris.

Although the quality *par excellence* began to depreciate, the more popular mass-produced automata were imported to England in considerable quantities.

These automaton toys of the Victorian era were frequently sold under glass shades, with the musical movement fitted into the velvet-covered wooden base. Those modelled as human figures performed naturalistic actions of head, eyes, mouth and limbs as in the examples of the waltzers, the snake charmer and the rope dancer. But the Victorian sense of humour is very evident in their toys. Not only did they make realistic human and animal automata, but they also delighted in motivating their animals to perform human tricks, as in the monkey artist, the monkey musician and the drinking bears. The variety of actions, occupations, tricks and surprises shown in these mechanical pieces affords both amusement and scope for today's collector. (If the figure has stood for many years on the covering of the base, the colour will probably have faded and a clear imprint of the base of the figure will remain – a good point to remember when estimating age).

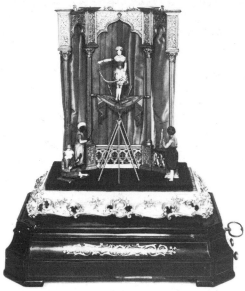

Left
Rope dancing automaton: key-wind musical playing two airs; push rod stop/start. Height without shade but including box 22½in

The central figure dances on a rope stretched 5½in above the velvet covered stage. She performs in time to the music: whilst her head moves up and down, her arms and legs stretch from left to right in a balancing act; she alights with perfect timing upon the spiked heel of her tiny foot. She is dressed in a gold-studded costume.

Height: 4¾in

Accompanying her are three musicians in oriental costume: on the left, a conductor (height 4½in) and a mandolin player (height 2½in seated), on the right a triangle player (height 4½in); each moves his head whilst his right hand plays the instrument.

Above
Monkey artist: key-wind; string-wind to musical box playing two airs; push rod stop/start. The artist's right arm holding the brush moves across the canvas; simultaneously he moves head, lower jaw, lip and eyes.

Last quarter of 19th century/French/Height from pergola top and including base: 20in

Above
The waltzers: key-wind musical; lever stop/start. The lady wears a violet crinoline, her partner a green satin coat and red breeches. The three-wheeled circular base, hidden beneath the crinoline, enables the figures to move in a circle and contains the musical movement; both figures gyrate upon the base. A metal label attached to the box reads 'A. THEROUDE. PARIS'.

Late 19th century/French/Height: 12½in

Left
Snake charmer or *La charmeuse au serpent*: handle-wind musical, push rod stop/start. This graceful oriental girl moves her head slowly whilst opening and closing her eyes; her right arm brings the trumpet across to her lips, whilst the head of the snake moves by the action of her left forearm. Her chest rises and falls rhythmically in perfect imitation of breathing. She is dressed in a green and gold costume with yellow sash; metal bracelets hide the joins where the arm movement occurs.
The snake is woven from realistically painted straw.
This model is reputed to be the first automaton designed and made by Gaston Decamps of Paris.

Height excluding box: 28½in

The preoccupation with monkeys as entertainment is a curious slant on the nineteenth century. Monkeys were amongst the earliest exhibits of the Zoological Society of London, which by 1835 showed many different examples including chimpanzees. It would follow, therefore, that from the middle of the nineteenth century monkeys could be seen and admired by greater numbers than ever before. Previously, collections of exotic animals had only existed in the private menageries of the aristocracy. Presumably the great zoos of Europe also received consignments of monkeys at roughly the same period, and this may account for the increasing popularity of the monkey as a toy.

The list of actions which these mechanical monkeys performed is extensive. They were made as drinkers, smokers, musicians, conjurors, drummers, artists, barbers, fishermen, and were often set within a pergola.

The quality of automata invented to divert the richer citizens of the eighteenth century was far removed from that produced for the less affluent Victorian living-room or nursery. The curiosities sold to ordinary families had an odd, humorous appeal and the greatest variety of the nineteenth century automata appeared in the range that depicted humans performing human actions, rather than that showing animals imitating humans.

Each generation has its speciality: steam, internal combustion, electricity – for the Victorians it must surely have been clockwork. With keys, cams, levers and springs they could make anything move – and they did! Artistes danced, ladies breathed, powdered, poured tea, rocked cradles and read books. Dandies smoked and took snuff, Grandma knitted and ironed, clowns and acrobats performed astonishing tricks. It is this range of imitative movement which attracts collectors, and as the figures were also beautifully dressed and accompanied by music, it is no wonder that they are as popular today as they were in the 1880s – though considerably more expensive.

Groups as well as single figures were made; these could sometimes be humorous, as for example 'The photographer and the reluctant sitter', where the sitter puts a pig's mask to her face as he attempts to take her portrait; and they would sometimes represent man in his everyday activities – five labourers building a church, three workmen in a village forge, children riding a carousel, and so on.

Except in what might be termed 'quality'

pieces, the musical movements were not elaborate, though they sometimes matched the action, for example a waltz for dancers. Following Edison's patent of the phonograph in 1877, the musical box proper declined, but the simple movements made for automata continued in production. The paper label stuck onto the base of many pieces gave only the titles of the music played, indicating that they could be supplied with a choice of tunes. (Collectors must be sure that a nineteenth century automaton is not accompanied by a tune of a much later date).

The keys for these mechanical pieces can sometimes help to identify the maker. Lucien Bontemps reputedly marked his keys with the initials 'L.B.' as part of the design of the key. Although old clock keys will often fit as a replacement for the original, most automata keys were not made of brass.

It should be noted that whilst it is possible to find figures performing many human actions, writing and drawing automata are rare and expensive.

The automata inventors strove to represent human actions and to imitate the natural behaviour of birds and animals – as distinct from a monkey playing a fiddle! Birds were an obvious choice. Not only were they decorative, with colourful plumage, but their song could be incorporated as the musical accompaniment. The sound of bird song reproduced by bird organs advanced with the technical brilliance of Jaquet Droz and Leschot, Maillardet, Rochat of Switzerland and others. Bontemps of Paris later made excellent movements for bird song.

Caged birds have an ancient association with man, so a singing bird in a gilded cage was clearly appropriate and if it could be made to 'fly' and perch, so much the better. The early boxes incorporating tiny singing birds gave way to the ornamental cages of the nineteenth century, with gilt-gesso base. The number of birds varied. The cages were designed with round, square, or octagonal bases, copying the real cages with perch and small door for insertion of food and water. Handles were large and solid, suitable for hanging or carrying. The exquisite pieces by Carl Fabergé were the playthings of the rich, but toy singing birds became so popular that

Monkey musician: key-wind; string-wind to musical box playing two airs; push rod stop/start. The violinist moves head, eyes and mouth whilst his 'bowing' arm moves across the strings.

Last quarter of 19th century/French/Height from pergola top and including base: 24½in

The dress is important. The originals wore silk knee-breeches, gold-braided coats and round velvet caps. The majority had head, eye, mouth, lip and limb movements, more intricate in the case of smokers. But the manufacturers also 'set the scene': the artist had perspective stick, portfolio, paints and wine bottle, the conjuror had a well-dressed table, and the musician had music-stand, score and violin case.

Near left
Cat boot-black: key-wind; non-musical; push rod stop/start. He is made with white fur covering a cardboard frame; he moves his head up and down whilst the right arm moves to and fro as in polishing.

Above
Drinking bear: key-wind musical; push rod stop/start. He moves his head up and down whilst opening and closing his jaws; the left arm raises and lowers the cup to mouth, whilst the right arm makes a cross-over movement from the joint to fill the cup. The liquid runs down the arm as the cup reaches the mouth and thence into the other arm to enter the flask for repouring.

c 1900/French/Height: 17in

Drumming bear: non-musical; key-wind; push rod stop/start. He moves his head sideways whilst opening and closing his jaw; both arms beat the drum vigorously.

c 1900/French/Height: 15½in

Since performing bears were common in England from Tudor times, it is not surprising that bears became the subjects for animated toys. They also had a long history as carved wooden toys in Europe. The automaton bears were made from cheap fur covering a cardboard or papier mâché frame, those containing a musical movement being slightly larger.

Right
Lady powderer: key-wind musical, playing two airs; push rod stop/start. Her bisque head turns and both arms move from the elbow joint. The lace-trimmed, silken open robe resembles an earlier fashion. The key bears the monogram 'L.B.' for Lucien Bontemps.

Early 20th century/French/Height: doll 15in; box 5in

Above
Spanish dancer: key-wind musical; push rod stop/start. This energetic little performer rotates upon her right foot, stamping her left foot in time to the music; her right arm moves from below the elbow joint as she shakes her tambourine and her head moves from side to side as she flirts her eyes. Dressed in yellow silk skirt and lace-trimmed, maroon velvet bodice.

c 1905/French (the doll head is German/Height: doll 16in; box 4in they were manufactured at varying prices – mainly in Switzerland, Germany and France – for export all over the world.

In England there appeared the additional embellishment of a penny-in-the-slot device to start the mechanism. Various cages were produced. The bases of the older types were frequently made of scrolled and gilded plaster-work; the later ones were of metal, whilst the Victorian ones were often mounted on a wooden support.

Making birds sing was one thing; making them walk and display was quite another. The peacock had long adorned noble estates and its outstanding appearance and grace were a challenge to the automata makers. Inevitably, the first imitations of this stately bird were unique and costly, but gradually their status descended in the social scale and eventually they became available to the general public. Real feathers were used instead of jewels and the mechanism was so well devised that as the bird walked its tail rose and fell, at the same time displaying the characteristic 'fan'.

Individual songsters and strutting peacocks did not, however, exhaust ideas for using automaton birds. They were produced in their natural setting of flowering trees and shrubs, called by collectors a 'bocage'. Groups such as these varied from two to nine birds and often included other automata – ducks swimming on a glass pool, a cascade of water, a windmill, a church tower or a rocking ship. Bontemps of Paris was one maker of these set pieces, many of which

Smoking chinaman: key-wind; non-musical; push rod stop/start. He turns his head as he smokes, lowering his eyelids and opening his mouth as he brings the pipe to his lips. Richly dressed in Oriental robes of yellow and patterned silk, with scarlet lining, collar and shoes.

c 1890/French/Height: 31in

By means of tubes and opening and closing bellows, a lighted cigarette placed in the bowl of the pipe will be smoked down to the stub and the smoke exhaled through the nostrils.

The carousel: Key-wind musical.
The octagonal box contains the musical movement and the roundabout has a central pillar with inset mirrors and eight silvered lamps. Beneath a colourful canopy, metal rods carry six riders mounted on white skin-covered horses. The dolls are bisque headed with real hair, and are dressed as boys and girls.

c 1910/French/Size: 21in high on base; dolls 4in

Cock and hen bird with fledglings: key-wind; lever stop/start. The delight of these birds is their natural trilling song. The metal label on base reads 'Ch. Bontems – Paris'.

Height with cage: 22in

Above
The bocage: key-wind; lever stop/start.
This model represents four birds grouped within a scene of rocks, flowering trees and waterfall. Only two have movement – the top bird and the one in the background remain stationary, whilst the lower bird dips its beak and drinks from the waterfall (a turning glass rod); the middle bird flutters from branch to branch.

Last quarter of 19th century/French/Height on base and without shade: 24in

When defeathered, these birds show an intricate metal mechanism. It is still possible to buy items from Victorian stuffed bird collections and feathers from these 'skins' are useful for minor repairs.

Right
The peacocks: non-musical; key-wind; lever stop/start.
These crested birds, with real peacock feathers, are descendants of the superb model by Fabergé. Both walk and display, the larger bird turning its neck from side to side. A simpler, more durable metal peacock was manufactured by Martin in 1880, and a German catalogue of the last century advertised a life-sized bird which could also scream!

c 1860/French/Size: 8in high, tail span 21in (large); 6in high, tail span 17in (small)

The crocodile: key-wind.
A lifelike toy of the post-war years with varnished and painted composition body, wooden legs and joint hinges of thin leather. It slithers along, moving lower jaw, legs and tail.

Length: 36in

Manufacturers offered other animal automata – disappearing rabbits, striped tigers, velvet pigs, cats, squirrels and growling dogs.

Above
The man in the moon: musical, playing two airs; key-wind; push rod stop/start.
This piece appears in German and French catalogues. Pierrot serenades the sickle moon. His right hand strums the mandolin and his tongue flicks in and out as he nods his head. The moon rolls his one large eye, opens and closes his mouth and sticks out his tongue. The musical movement is concealed behind the base of the papier mâché moon.

c 1890/French/Height from tip of moon: 19½in

The moon was also fashioned as a smoker, with the body of a man and the full moon as the smiling face.

Above
A negro automaton with the musical movement contained within the body. Key-wind with push rod stop/start and playing three airs. The composition head moves from side to side and up and down whilst the eyes blink. On his tray he carries an apple (at left) which opens to reveal a monkey head with eyelid and lip movement, a pear (centre) with dancing figures and a peach with a circling mouse. Dressed in pink brocade with gilt earrings and buttons.

Mid-19th century/French/Height: 26in

These blackamoors are quite rare, but there are examples of male and female figures.

were combined with a musical movement.

During the eighteenth century, elaborate animal automata were constructed for important personages, and animal figures continued to be made in ever-increasing quantities and with great variety of movement, though the quality never again approached the standard of the early works. They became, in fact, playthings rather than princely presents.

Some of the oddities in this strange world of automata were entirely fanciful and the man in the moon was the subject of several compositions. As ever, he was endowed by his makers with a human face and personality.

A whole series of mechanical pieces lay in the field of animated scenes and card pictures. These clockwork specimens were rivalled by those cranked by hand, somewhat cheaper but not necessarily of inferior workmanship. The figures were mounted upon a covered box and both musical and non-musical models were made.

The works of the masters – Jaquet Droz,

Houdin, Maillardet and Cox, to name but a few – are mostly in museums, but it is still possible to obtain examples by, amongst others, Decamps, Roullet, Theroude, Lucien Bontemps. Available too are a number of popular items made in the last quarter of the nineteenth century and exported by French, German and Swiss firms.

The makers of the purely mechanical parts of automata used heads from different suppliers. French and German doll heads were commonly used, not necessarily in their country of origin. Additionally, they sold their products in various foreign markets and one can find the same piece illustrated in many catalogues. The distributor usually omitted to mention the name of the actual maker and this makes identification most difficult, especially as one cannot disturb a delicately balanced head, nor push up the hair to identify the mark. One is grateful, therefore, to those makers who used distinctive keys, though this is no sure method of attribution since they could be removed and used with other pieces.

The collector buying automata today may have to be content with a figure that is imperfect and a musical movement that needs repair. This should not deter him; there are musical box restorers and figures can be refurbished. Fur-covered animals must be stripped down for repair and the coat cut, patched and restuck. Singing birds sometimes have to be refeathered, which is exacting but not impossible. It is a mistake to use too much oil as it tends to clog the works. So, too, do the hairs of the furred animals, which gradually get pushed down into the mechanism with each winding. Automata should never be left with the movement entirely run down.

The price today is affected by rarity and condition, but most pieces offered for sale have had to be repaired to some degree, and this in no way detracts from their appeal when they are finally shown in working order.

Left
Two hand-cranked musical toys. In both, the musical movement is in the box base. At top, a clown with a rearing pony which he flicks with a whip as the music plays. Below, a delightful tea party – two elegant silk-clad ladies take tea, whilst a maid passes from one to the other with the tea-pot. The ladies have head and arm movements and sip their tea as the music plays.

c 1910 (both)/German/Size: clown 9½in, box 11½ x 5 x 3½in; dolls 5½in, box 8½ x 11½ x 3in

Right
At top, the dog band: non-musical; key-wind. Seven cut-out cardboard dogs with head and arm movements play various musical instruments. There were many different subjects in this series – the example shown below is the man with mouse; he nods his head and strikes at a darting mouse which he never succeeds in hitting.

c 1880/1890/German/Size framed in glazed box: 14in x 10½in

Dolls

Doll-collecting has become so popular in Britain in recent years that it needs patience and diligent searching to gather a representative collection but, happily, it is still possible to find examples of early dolls showing the craftsmanship which is appreciated in all antiques.

Wood

One would like to be able to find dolls of the seventeenth and eighteenth centuries (then called 'babies') but this is not likely for the average collector, though they can be studied in museums and private collections. These very early types, sometimes called 'Queen Anne' dolls, were hand carved and later machine turned, with hair or animal-hair wigs, blown glass or painted eyes and rather highly coloured faces, looking one might say like 'painted ladies'. The other type of very early doll found today is the crèche doll which is not really a doll at all, but a carved religious figure or statue. They had finely modelled features and came from Catholic countries on the continent where there has always been a fine tradition of artist-craftsmen working for the Church.

However, many collectors begin with the so-called 'Dutch' (a corruption of Deutsch) or penny-wooden dolls and these are still obtainable but, unfortunately, not all are old – one should look for the carved indication of a nose and for the grey curls beneath the painted black head to be sure of a really old wooden doll. These dolls were very much nursery toys, bought cheaply and dressed from the work-box. They were produced in Austria and Germany and collectors will find great variation in size and quality. As a general rule, the older models were better finished with a comb carved at the top of the head.

Papier mâché

The doll-makers of the early nineteenth century were quick to follow the furniture-makers in their use of papier mâché and produced delightful doll heads of this material. They also used it as a base, finishing the process by dipping in wax.

Paper

Perhaps because of the flimsy nature of this material, few early examples have survived to be available for collectors today. The idea was simple – a one-dimensional cut-out card figure, slotted at the feet into a small wooden stand. On to this figure could be slipped a variety of dresses, hats and head-dresses (see Paper Toys.)

Wax

The English were famed for their wax dolls and fortunately these have survived in considerable quantities. An early type was the 'pumpkin head', where the hair, head, and bust were moulded in one, with pupilless brown glass eyes, and sometimes found with a hat or head-dress also moulded in wax.

The late Georgian and early Victorian dolls were commonly made of wax over composition, with wig attached through a

Above
Three early wooden dolls. At left, a carved oak doll with bosom exposed which might indicate that it was made in the pre-Cromwellian era.

Early 17th century/English/Height: 8½in

Centre, an oak stump doll with simple carved decoration showing the tall hat fashionable in the period of James 1.

Early 17th century/English/Height: 11¼in

Right shows a carved folk doll, probably home made, with painted red dress, black cloak and bonnet.

18th century/American/Height: 6½in

centre slit on the head (causing the cracks these early faces so often show). The eyes were fixed, or moved by manipulation of a wire through the body which was usually made of stuffed cotton or linen, more rarely of kid.

Another popular Victorian doll was of poured wax and had a more solid, sturdier appearance. The most expensive had each hair or group of hairs individually inserted into the hot wax, the wax head and shoulder plate being attached to the body by thread or fine string passing through eyelet holes.

Some of the most prized wax dolls were made by Montanari; other famous doll-makers were Pierotti and Marsh. The Montanaris are mostly unmarked, as are many wax dolls, but they have a sullen 'droop' to the mouth corners and the folds in the flesh are well moulded and markedly indicated.

The Victorian wax 'baby' dolls were remarkable for their beautifully hand-sewn clothes, replicas of the baby clothes of the period, and one wonders how such delicate creatures survived the hazards of nursery life. It was perhaps because they were usually played with only on Sundays and by the time their elaborate garments had been removed, the doll played with and then redressed, Sunday was over; consequently they escaped daily wear and tear.

A small but delightful class of wax doll are those made as portraits. These were faithfully modelled to the likeness of the subject and one of the most popular was that of the young Queen Victoria. These are rare and quite unmistakable when compared with contemporary prints and paintings.

Parian

The parian-headed dolls (white unglazed china) had hair and sometimes head-dresses moulded in one with the head and bust. The great majority had painted eyes; the rarer ones had inset glass eyes. These dolls have great delicacy, especially the smaller ones and, as in the glazed china types, the bodies are of stuffed cotton material or kid, with china limbs. A few bear the Meissen mark on the shoulder.

Glazed china

The various materials of which dolls were

Above
Two early wooden dolls. The heads, with hair wigs, are of gessoed wood with 'stitched' eyebrows, enamel eyes, carved fingers and jointed limbs. The one on the left has a head which can be moved by a rod through the body, and wears a closed robe of pink silk over a corset, blue silk shoes and fob watch. The one on the right is dressed in yellow silk over a quilted petticoat and corset. It has a leading string attached to the right shoulder (originally there would have been two for an adult to hold and keep the child upright) – hence the expression 'being in leading strings'.

Left c 1745/1765/English/Height: 20½in
Right c 1765/1775/English/Height: 20in

Right
Two papier mâché-headed dolls. The standing doll has painted features with modelled hair and is of the type which some collectors call 'Pandora'. The body and limbs are stuffed and the gown is of glazed fawn cotton.

c 1830/English/Height: 20in

The seated doll has glass eyes and bamboo teeth. The head has painted black hair beneath the hair wig which can be attached through two nail holes on the head. The body is of pink kid and the limbs are not articulated. Dressed in striped silk dress, green cloak and straw bonnet. This type of doll is sometimes called a 'Milliner's Model'.

c 1845/French/Height: 15½in

Above
At left, a fine wooden doll with gesso head. The delicately painted features include 'stitched' eyebrows and short black curls. The body is fully jointed with shaped legs and carved fingers. Dressed in cream cotton dress with gauze trimming and matching hat.

c 1815/1820/English/Height: 16in

Centre seated and right are two 'Dutch' dolls with painted features. The larger has ball and socket joints and the smaller has peg joints at elbows, thighs and knees.

Late 19th century/German/Height: large 21½in; small 12in

Above
Two wax over composition dolls. The standing doll has hair and plumed hat moulded in wax, with pupilless glass eyes, stuffed body with squeak box, wooden legs and 'spoon' hands.

c 1850/60/English/Height: 18in

Seated is a two-faced doll by Bartenstein. A pull-string through the stiffened cylindrical body enables either a crying or a smiling face to appear beneath the fixed hood which is covered by a bonnet. The limbs are wax over composition.

c 1880/German/Height: 1ft 2in

A group of unusual wax dolls. At left, two fashion dolls with wax heads on kid bodies charmingly dressed in satin and silk, with parasols and elaborate hats. The wax heads have painted features and real hair wigs.

Edwardian/English/Height: 1ft 2in

At right is a wax mask doll. The face only is of wax – the back of the head is of padded cloth. The head has pin-sized glass pupils in the eyes and one curl of blonde hair fixed beneath the bonnet. The stuffed body has cloth limbs and the box, which bears the inscription 'A present from Lady Granville to dear little Mary – Oct. 14 1854', also has the legend 'Montanari Doll' on one side.

c 1854/English/Height: 13in

Above
Two parian dolls. At left, a fine quality doll with moulded blonde hair and ribbon through the curls. She has inset blue glass eyes and glass earrings. The arms and legs are of china with glazed painted boots.

c 1875/European/Height: 10in

At right, a larger parian head with moulded blonde hair and painted eyes. The stuffed body has china arms and legs with black painted boots.

c 1880/Probably English/Height: 18in

Left
Two poured wax dolls. At left, a Montanari portrait doll of Queen Victoria's eldest daughter. The hair is inserted singly, the eyes are blue glass and the stuffed body has wax limbs attached through eyelet holes. The wax moulding shows chubby folds of 'flesh' and the mouth droops.

Mid-19th century/English/Height: 1ft 9 in

At right, a Pierotti baby doll with red-brown hair inserted in tufts. The eyes are blue glass and the wax has a mauve tinge. The stuffed body has wax limbs attached through eyelet holes. The Pierotti family probably had the longest history of wax doll-making in England. Dressed in white embroidered dress.

Last quarter of 19th century/English/Height: 19in

Above
Two glazed china-headed dolls. The one on the right has moulded black hair, stuffed body and china limbs, with black painted slippers. There is a faint red line above the eye.

c 1840-1860/German/Height: 22in

The doll on the left has glazed blonde moulded hair, blue eyes and china limbs attached to the stuffed body. Dressed in blue silk with muslin bodice and overskirt.

c 1880/German/Height: 13in

made fall only approximately into different dates. Roughly the sequence is: wood, wax, papier mâché, glazed china, parian and bisque – but, of course, some manufacturers continued to use a certain material long after others were trying something new. But it is fairly safe to say that the glazed china heads followed the wax ones, and many have survived in very good condition. They are recognisable by their black hair, modelled in one with head and bust, and almost always they represent a girl or woman with adult clothing.

They have the sedate air of a bygone age, with arms, hands and legs also of china. The earlier ones have sloping shoulders, a faint red line over the eyelid and painted slippers, whilst the later ones have the button boots of late Victorian times.

Bisque

This type of doll is named after the 'biscuit' stage of china-making (when the paste is first fired and left unglazed), and these lovely heads are the ones which are most commonly seen or remembered. They were made in France and Germany up to World War I and it is of bisque that most automata dolls' heads are made. Many bisque-headed dolls have the maker's name or mark on the back of the head, neck, shoulder or body. The eyes were fixed in earlier models, followed by sleeping and flirting eyes. There were many famous French and German makers of bisque heads, the Jumeau dolls being noted for their large, brilliant eyes. Perhaps one of the most frequently found marks today is A.M. for Armand Marseille and, whilst these are not rare, they should be included in a collection.

The life-like colouring and delicate modelling produced a doll which is still unsurpassed for excellence of craftsmanship. The earlier ones had kid bodies, the limb joints beautifully gusseted and stitched. The later bodies were of composition, with ball and socket joints and elastic stringing. The earlier heads were made in one with the shoulder, with closed mouths and often with pierced ears for the addition of earrings. Later came the swivel heads and open mouths, sometimes showing teeth. These elaborately dressed 'fashion' dolls, as illustrated on the right, were luxury toys and could be bought with elegant costumes and accessories. The bodies could be of stuffed cloth, fine kid, or wood, the latter having the advantage of fully jointed limbs.

Restoration Those who have handled restored and unrestored dolls prefer those which retain their own peculiar appeal and wear the scars of age. When an old doll has been rewigged, repainted and redressed, it has lost all its character and most of its charm. Good advice would be 'make good and mend' doing as little as possible and using old materials and hand sewing.

Fakes With rising prices there are many fakes on the market. Look out for badly stuck modern nylon wigs, soft glove-kid bodies of a chalk whiteness, oddly proportioned bodies and machine-stitched clothes of old materials.

Above
A bisque-headed Parisienne with swivel neck, fixed blue eyes, a blonde wool wig and kid arms on a stuffed stockinette body, wearing a green silk gown edged with black velvet.

c 1865/French/Height: 16in

Left

A group of dolls showing different materials. At left, a celluloid baby doll with painted features. This material had a high fire risk and was discontinued for dolls – hence the rhyme: 'If there's a toy you must avoid, it is the one of celluloid'.

c 1920/Japanese/Height: 22in

The baby doll at right, with stuffed body and painted muslin head, is by Kathe Kruse and bears the original label round the neck. It was intended to represent a real baby, with lolling head and rounded limbs.

c 1920/German/Height: 20in

Seated is a doll with stuffed body, metal head, wooden forearms and painted features.

c 1922/German/Height: 17in

At left by chair is a small doll with composition head and rubber body. Although rubber was unbreakable, it eventually perished and rubber dolls in good condition are not easy to find.

c 1920–1930/English/Height: 10in

Above

Two marked bisque dolls with fixed eyes, closed mouths and composition bodies. At left, a Bru head; at right, a Jumeau.

Late 19th century/French/Height: Bru 28in; Jumeau 22in

Dolls' Clothing, Accessories, and Miniature Ware

Dolls' clothing

The wooden dolls of the mid-eighteenth and early nineteenth century had hand-made clothes of fine needlework in the materials and styles of an adult of that period. If the doll was made to represent a lady, it would have the exact copy of a corset, with whalebone, lace-holes and embroidery. If it was intended to represent a child, it would still be wearing clothes of adult style – since children's clothes of that time were copies of their elders'.

Items of male doll clothing have not survived in great numbers. Moth damage made greater inroads on wools and worsteads and very young boys and girls dressed similarly – a boy being identifiable by his clothes only when he was old enough to be 'breeched'.

The Dutch dolls, or penny-woodens, were admirably suited for dressing at home. Small, durable and cheap, they could be inexpensively clothed from scraps, often with pieces left over from their owners' dresses. These are the small dolls which Queen Victoria dressed in her childhood, and sewing for these unpretentious dolls must have been a nursery pastime for more than 150 years.

When dolls were individually made, or manufactured in small numbers, their clothes, too, were hand made at home or by the dressmaker. With the mass-production of dolls – the waxes of England and the continental bisques – dolls' clothing also was manufactured on a larger scale. This type of employment was very suitable for outworkers, and the underpaid and overworked employees in the sweat shops of Victorian England (many of them children themselves) must have been responsible for many of the cheap but finely sewn articles of dolls' clothing.

In Europe, particularly in France, the clothes and accessories of the expensive dolls were made with the same care and attention to detail as was lavished on the fashionable wardrobe of an adult.

The 1900s and the idea of making dolls to represent babies and young children brought a change of style. Dolls began to look more like their owners and less like great ladies. Many now wore black stockings, button boots and the white starched pinafore so representative of the early years of this century.

Dating dolls is made easier if they still wear their original clothes, and possessing dolls with authentic clothing is a delight for any collector – unfortunately, this also puts up the price!

Toy miniature ware

Miniature ware for table and bedroom use was made in many sizes. Some was scaled to fit into dolls' houses and other half-services were manufactured and decorated especially for children. Small-scale toy vessels of pottery and earthenware have been excavated from ancient sites, but one cannot be certain if these miniature domestic objects were for child-play or had a religious significance.

Before the specialist toyshop came into existence, the bazaars selling toys and fancy goods attracted the richer customer, whilst children with only a penny or two bought from street sellers. Dolls' bedsteads were hawked through the streets of early Victorian London with the cry:

'Doll's bedsteads, is my daily cry;
Ye misses, come and choose;
Such sorts and sizes I have here,
To buy you'll not refuse'.

In shrill tones the pedlars sought the custom of young boys, their cries advertising 'flags, swords, or windmills O!'

'Come, my young masters, come to me,
I've flags both red and blue;
One penny is the price of them –
My swords are well worth two'.

Today, the most likely finds for a collector of toy table ware will be the services, part-services and boxed sets of the late nineteenth and early twentieth centuries. Identification is not easy as most pieces were unmarked in the cheaper ranges; however, the pattern books of some manufacturers do show miniature ware and very often the small items followed the design of the full-scale pieces, so the shape of jugs, teapots, and so on can be a useful guide.

Many toy tea-sets came from Germany, but English makers came to the fore after World War I and Japanese imports increased. The kitchen sets (page 58), like the first model kitchens from Nuremberg, were educational toys as well as delightful playthings. Every little girl's ambition was to

Above
A doll's trunk from America. The trunk, properly made of leather, studded and papered inside with roses, contained not only the more usual items of clothing, hats, shoes, stays, etc, but fans, jewellery and a delightful bustle to tie round the waist and achieve the correct line *à derrière*! In one of the trunk's compartments was the ultimate item for a true lady of fashion – a black face mask for wearing to the grand ball.

c 1870/American

Above
A loose-leaved book containing the work of Sophie Golden, aged sixteen years, a pupil of 'Westgate House, Peterborough. Conducted by Miss Willoughby'. Tacked to its pages are dolls' garments exhibiting the very finest sewing. Tucks, hems and trimmings are all hand done with stitches almost too fine to see. There are six items: bodice, petticoat, nightdress, waist petticoat and drawers, and a 3in sample of white work. Such excellence would have been difficult to achieve in a full-sized garment – on dolls' clothes of 4-8ins, with cuffs only ½in wide, it must have been an almost superhuman task.

c 1892/English

Above
Dolls' tea-set, decorated with dark blue rim and gold stars.

Early 20th century/English/Size: Jug 2¾in

Tea-parties were a great part of middle-class English life and pouring tea from a 'real' china service was often a little girl's first attempt at imitating one of Mama's social occasions.

Above
Everything for a lady of fashion: ribbons, eyeglass on gilt chain; boots for the country, satin shoes for town wear and cream silk shoes for the bride; a black umbrella, long kid gloves and a clothes-brush; travelling sets of brush, mirror and comb; hair combs and curling-tongs; a small boxed handkerchief and a beautiful cream lace and chiffon hat for the bride. Centre is a black ostrich feather fan on tortoiseshell mounts.

c 1860-1910/English and French/Various sizes

Above
A wooden box containing a dinner service for two of Britannia metal. The items are: eight plates, cruet frame, knife rests, bowl, tureen, napkin rings, candlesticks, beakers and cutlery. The box label bears the firm's mark 'C.B.G.', showing the award of a silver medal in 1878 and a gold in 1900.

c 1875/French/Size: 7¼ x 10½in

Above
Dolls' nine-piece bedroom set with blue/mauve decoration, including basin and ewer, pail, chamber pot, soap dish, tooth-brush holder.

Early 20th century/English/Size: jug 5½in

Many houses had very inadequate bathroom facilities and this set exemplifies in miniature the sort of equipment which would have been found in most bedrooms throughout Victorian and Edwardian times.

have miniature copies of kitchen utensils, filled with rice or 'pretend' food, to cook for a family of dolls. Stoves, too, came in various materials (japanned tin-plate, cast iron etc) and in assorted sizes. Some were small enough to fit into a dolls' house and others were capable of giving a gentle heat and of being used for cooking. With stove-pipe, opening oven doors and miniature utensils, they really worked and, like the toy sewing machines, gave some result for hard labour!

An interesting development of the toy-sized sets were the 'baby sets'. These, according to the *British Toymaker* of 1915, 'comprised four pieces: a deep porridge plate, a small tea plate, and a cup and saucer'. They were 'suitable for presentation to a small child for actual use' and, at the same time, they were 'capable of being alternatively used as a toy'. They were supplied unboxed

and showed nursery motifs.

These baby sets continue to be produced and those of comparatively recent years depict popular characters – the Beatrix Potter favourites, etc. They make a decorative addition to a toy collection, are easily found and can only increase in value and interest.

Hints for collectors You can assemble and design your own display from items in your collection. An attractive way to present a variety of small items is to position them on polystyrene ceiling tiles and attach them with nylon fishing line or invisible thread. Do not use glue – other than purpose-made – or it will react with the polystyrene. (The method recommended is especially useful if you travel and lecture with these examples.)

Above
Dolls' dinner service prettily decorated with rose border, showing part of a service for twelve; this was probably a set for grand occasions.

Early 20th century/English/Size: tureen 6in long

Above
A blue enamel on tin kitchen set of twelve pieces, including pots, pans, ladles, slices and fish mould.

Early 20th century

Mechanical Dolls and Novelties

Dolls were man's first attempt to fashion a lifelike toy and it became a challenge to make dolls which could imitate the movements of the human body. Necessarily, this refinement in manufacture was only possible for firms dealing in the more expensive items and many attempts were neither wholly successful nor commercially viable.

This art of imitation is still with us and every Christmas brings its crop of action dolls which can walk, talk, cry and drink. The early mechanical dolls could not perform such a wide range of actions, but the charm of the Victorian mechanical dolls has not been surpassed, chiefly because their makers used fine quality bisque heads – Jumeau being one example.

The early, simple movements were rod and string operated; for example, the eye movements were effected by a wire or strings through the body which, when pulled, could present a head with crying, smiling or sleeping face. Strings also activated voice boxes to say 'Mama' or 'Papa'.

It is obvious that the solid bodies of the earlier dolls could not enclose the mechanism either for motivation or for music which the hollow, carton-like bodies of later dolls could easily accommodate. Very often, therefore, bodies for mechanical dolls had to be specially constructed.

Other than rods and strings, clockwork initiated the greatest range of simulated movement. Many manufacturers attempted the walking doll, one of the most famous being the American Autoperipatetikos of 1862. Another famous walking doll was that made by Steiner at the turn of the century. It could sit and walk, but the walking was not entirely independent; the doll had to be hand-held. Jules Steiner made yet another walking doll which, like the Autoperipatetikos, had a cardboard cone beneath the skirt which concealed the mechanism. He also made talking dolls, but one must remember that the vocabulary of the talking dolls was usually restricted to 'Mama' and 'Papa'.

In addition to the opening-closing, sleeping eye-movement, makers tried the sideways or flirting eye-movement. Two manufacturers, amongst others, were Simon & Halbig, and Kammer & Reinhardt. After about 1912, even a tongue movement was available. For instance one doll with a Jumeau head, which seemingly poured and drank coffee had a tongue imitating a tasting movement.

Collectors should also try to include a marotte (page 60).

Swimming dolls fetch high prices at auction, particularly the French doll by Martin, named 'Ondine' or water sprite, of 1876. It had a cork body and wooden arms and legs. Crawling babies were also attempted; Clay in the U.S.A. and Newton in England both made these in the 1870s. Key wound, they crawled along moving their heads from side to side. Besides crawling, walking and talking, dolls were made to blow kisses, to cry, jump, recite, sing, breathe, telephone, run and fall, feed, bathe, blow bubbles and hop!

A famous talking doll was the Edison phonograph doll of the late nineteenth century, wound by a handle at the back. Jumeau

Above
Two Autoperipatetikos dolls. The one on the left has a delicate bisque head with moulded blonde hair and painted features. The upper detail of the bodice and gilt-edged collar are also moulded in china. The dress is of mauve and cream silk.

Height: 11in

On the right is a cloth-headed example with painted features and hair. This type often turned out to be better performers than the china – or bisque-headed dolls, perhaps because the cloth head was lighter in weight.

c 1862/American/Height: 10in

also made a phonograph doll with interchangeable cylinders.

Most collectors try to include a multifaced doll. These were popular in the late nineteenth century and there were several makers. The faces not on show were concealed by a cardboard hood and each face came into view by turning a screw protruding through the bonnet trimming. Probably the mark most frequently found are the initials C.B. for Carl Bergner. The Bru turning face is perhaps the most sought-after model, but there were other makers including Joanny, Faugier and Checkeni of the U.S.A.

Perhaps the most famous feeding doll was Bru's 'Bébé Têteur', worked by a key and suction movement which emptied and returned the liquid into the feeding bottle. Leidel of Germany and Steiner both patented nursing dolls and, although the imitation of drinking was a novelty, the action, whether by suction or syphon, was never entirely satisfactorily resolved. Surviving working examples are rare, because parts of the mechanism were made of perishable rubber.

Doll enthusiasts are not always automata collectors, but many will want to include mechanical examples. With the present-day promotion of toys, it is likely that dolls will become even more imitative and that transistorised mechanisms will enable manufacturers to produce all sorts of actions which the early doll-makers could not achieve. It is certainly worthwhile buying one or two modern examples, as well as searching for the old ones – they can only appreciate in value. Nowadays, they are likely to be of Swiss or Japanese manufacture and each Christmas brings new inventors. It is a long road from the Grecian jointed doll of the fifth century BC to the toy moon-walkers of the present era, but every age shows man's efforts to produce something truly lifelike in his own image.

Note for collectors Some mechanical dolls are bought with good original clothes, others need repair. Redressing a mechanical doll is not easy. Collars have to be loose for neck movement, sleeves sometimes need to be stitched on to the outside armhole edge and the whole costume has to be removable or at least detachable in part to make repairs possible. Repairs are another problem. In England one has to wait months to obtain the services of the few excellent repairers of mechanical dolls or automata, though watch-menders will sometimes oblige. Prices are highly competitive.

This is a field where, perhaps, condition competes with rarity. Sometimes one can find a good piece in poor repair and have it mended, but for the average collector of intricate mechanical pieces, condition is the most important factor.

Above
At left, a marotte or musical rattle. This toy was for a baby but would have been twirled on its stick by an adult, for it is quite heavy. The music is in the round body which is surmounted by a small bisque head. Many marottes had bells attached.

c 1895/French/Height on stick: 12in

At right, a fortune-telling doll of wood with a pleated paper skirt. Each pleat is shaped like a folded petal and opens to reveal a hand-written fortune. The coloured paper pleats were probably cut commercially and sold for home assembly, where appropriate fortunes could be written by hand on each pleat. The triangular slips of paper were of different colours and threaded on a string tied round the waist. The opened pleat shown here carries this slightly critical message: 'You are a little flirting elf – you talk of nothing but Yourself.'

Above
A mechanical doll by Jules Steiner, the *Bébé Premier Pas*. Key wound at the thigh; it had to be hand held whilst it walked. The elaborate clothes of white and blue are dotted with gilt beads and the matching hat is feather trimmed. The eyes are without lashes and the open mouth shows the little pointed teeth so typical of many Steiner dolls.

c 1890/Patented in France/Height: 18in

Right
A singing doll by Webber of America. The wax over composition head has real hair and fixed glass eyes, and the arms are kid with separate fingers. The stuffed body held the mechanism which was operated by pressing the central wooden button. There were a variety of sizes and songs available – stamped across the body of this one is 'I sing Happy Land'.

c 1884/American/Height: 27in

Above
A walking and talking doll bearing the label 'Cremers, Game & Toy Warehouse, 22 New Bond Street'. It represents a young child and has articulated bisque arms which move up and down as it walks along calling 'Mama' and 'Papa'. It is mounted on a circular base with three wheels, the front one operated by a cam causing the doll to change the direction of its forward movement.

c 1890/Doll probably by Steiner/Height: 15½in

Above
A swimming doll similar to the Martin doll, but unmarked. The body is constructed of two cork slabs with the clockwork mechanism fitted between, enabling her to perform a most realistic breast stroke. She has a German bisque head, metal hands and jointed wooden legs and wears the conventional high-buttoning bathing dress of the late Victorian period.

Late 19th century/Length: 14½in

Note: Swimming dolls should not be confused with bathing dolls, which were small china dolls without moving limbs (also known as 'frozen charlottes') which could be safely bathed or washed.

Right
A walking and talking child doll by Jumeau, with bisque head, blonde mohair wig, brown sleeping eyes, open mouth and heavy brows. The body and limbs are of composition and wood, the arms jointed at shoulder, wrist and elbow, with the lower arms moving on a riveted pin. As the doll is walked along, her head turns from side to side and she cries 'Mama'. She wears an original dress of pink satin, matching straw hat, pink socks and white shoes.

Early 20th century/French/Height: 21½in

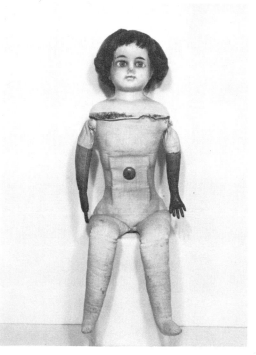

Money Pots and Boxes

Pottery, Wood and Metal

Thrift was a Victorian ideal and there are many proverbs and sayings to instil this virtue 'A penny saved is a penny earned'. Money boxes were especially popular presents from adults to children. They were given as toys and also displayed on shop counters so that customers could donate coins from their change to a deserving charity. Traditionally, money boxes were opened and their contents distributed to the poor on the day after Christmas – Boxing Day.

Since early times, people have put their savings into a pot or jar; much later the container became a box. The very cheap pottery ones which had to be destroyed to obtain the contents have obviously not survived, but the more decorative types, which were regarded as ornaments as well as banks and fashioned as animals, fruits etc, are still available. They are not sought after as are the tin or mechanical banks of cast iron, and are therefore cheaper in price. The mechanical banks have become recognised collectors' items, and tend to be expensive.

The reason for the design of a pig as a savings pot is uncertain. Pigs were certainly part of a countryman's wealth and a piggin or 'pig' is an old word for an earthenware vessel or pot. Money boxes shaped as pigs remain common, and equally popular were money boxes made as hens with chicks – protecting the savings or nest-egg.

Getting at the money was another matter! Apart from smashing the container, the time-honoured custom of inserting a knife blade into the money slot was known to every child. The metal banks, however, either had strategic screws, so that the bank could be taken apart, the contents emptied and the bank used again, or they were simply opened by means of lock and key.

Familiarity made toys beloved; anticipation and surprise kept them in use. That is why mechanical banks surpassed the still-life type in popularity. A child knew, after the first insertion of a coin, that something exciting and unexpected was going to happen and yet he wanted to see the performance over and over again (another penny saved!). So the oddities of the mechanical banks displayed great ingenuity of design – William Tell shooting the apple, Jonah and the whale, Paddy and his pig and so on.

Above
The green glazed pottery hen and chicks decorate a pot bank with slot in the base. The Welsh inscription reads: 'A silver key opens every lock'.

c 1880/Welsh/(Ewenni pottery)/Height: 7½in

The wooden 'POOR' box belonged to a child of nine who was expected to collect from her friends for less fortunate children.

c 1866/English/Size: 5 x 3 x 1¾in

The 'turret' box, with slot in the removable top, blue transfer flower print and legend 'Bank – The Pennies Make the Pounds', is an example of the small wooden souvenirs made at Mauchline in Ayrshire.

Early 20th century/Scottish/Height: 3½in

Above
Three cast iron banks: all unscrew to open. The grotesque painted figure perhaps represents the golliwog.

c 1910/English/Height: 6½in

The Georgian house bank with brass decoration is found with a coin or a sun motif above the central money slot. (Do not date the bank by the coin, which can be soldered in place).

Late 18th century/English/Height: 7½in

The small house bank with money slot beneath the roof is typical of many British and American iron toys. It has pierced decorations at the sides to enable the saver to watch his money accumulating.

Mid-19th century/Height: 3in

Left
Four novelty tin boxes dating to the first half of the twentieth century. The painted 'combination' safe with money slot at the back was designed to make the withdrawal of money marginally difficult.

English/Size: 6 x 3½ x 3½in

The cash register has a spring-loaded drawer at base and a money slot at top.

American/Height: 4½in

The fireplace is painted with simulated coal fire and has a money slot at the top.

English/Height: 4½in

The top hat has the money slot beneath the brim. It was an obvious design for a savings bank, as traditionally the hat was used as a receptacle for alms.

Above
Three mechanical cast iron banks dating to the latter half of the nineteenth century. The owl moves his head when a lever is depressed and the coin drops through the slot at the neck.

Height: 8in

The seated figure represents the American politician, William Tweed, who was reputed to accept bribes. When a coin is put into the right hand, he lowers it into his pocket – a slot concealed by the bent left arm.

Height: 6½in

The negro puts the coin to his mouth and 'swallows' it when a lever is depressed, meanwhile blinking his eyes.

Height: 6in

Optical Toys

Perhaps more than anything else, optical toys give to the viewer the experience of another dimension and the illusion of movement. As collectors' items they are especially interesting because from these humble beginnings (allied to the camera and whatever source of lighting was available) developed all the refinements of today's great motion picture industry.

Whilst navigational aids – the telescope, the microscope and surveying instruments such as the theodolite – must be considered as optical antiques, other variations in the optical field were specifically made as toys. The development of optical science is not as modern as one might suppose. The zoetrope for instance, popular in the 1860s, was the forerunner of today's cartoons and a Dutchman pioneered magic lantern projection as long ago as 1660. Scientific instruments, such as simple microscopes and various optical toys, could not be bought with pocket money, but they were rightly considered as first class educational toys and were eagerly purchased and presented by Victorian parents. Moving shadows needed no money and every home could have them!

Shadows
The ancient method of animation by shadow was oriental in origin and almost universal in practice. The Chinese gave artistic performances of shadow plays and from this old idea developed the cut-out silhouette sheets of the nineteenth century. The principle is still with us. What child has not been delighted by the lifelike effect produced by throwing the shadow of his hands upon a wall? The outlines of a rabbit, dog, butterfly etc could all be produced with the fingers and thumb entwined to make the required features.

Peep-shows
There were, of course, purely mechanical means of giving the impression of depth, distance and change of position – the peep-show is one. Originally a public entertainment in the seventeenth century, models were later made as toys and modifications of this type of dimensional viewing toy were made of paper to commemorate the building of the Thames tunnel; variations continued in production for many years afterwards.

Above
A detail from an engraving by John Burnet of a painting by David Wilkie (1816). Note the source of light – a candle held by the child on the extreme left. The print also shows the interior of a rural home and the simplicity of the amusements which a poorer family could afford.

Right
A triangular section peep-show in mahogany cabinet with a viewing hole at each side, showing a soirée and banquet in a pillared room with mirror walls. The mirrors give the effect of a throng of fashionablly dressed ladies and gentlemen either being received or seated at the banqueting table. There are in fact twenty-nine carved and painted wooden figures, all under 1in high.

The box is 12in wide, 6¼in high, with viewing holes of 1¼in diameter.

c 1790/English

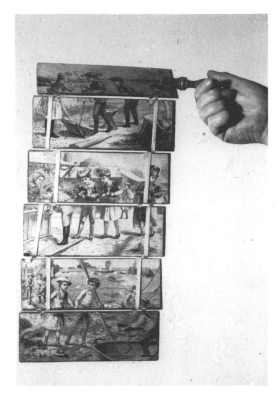

Above

A hand-coloured pull-out paper and card toy of the Thames tunnel. There are three viewing holes: the one at centre top gives a view of the busy river scene in full colour, a glimpse of old London on the left and many rowing boats and sailing ships bedecked with flags. The bottom viewing holes show the marvels of the tunnel beneath the river, with arching roof, foot travellers, stall holders etc. It was probably sold as a souvenir.

The card box lid, which is an integral part of the toy, measures 7½in wide by 6½in, and the tunnel, fully extended, measures 21in.

c 1840/43/English

Above

Changing picture toy. Each complete picture consists of two sections 7in x 2½in; the set of six sections gives three pictures. Illustrated is the artist, the fair and the boating party – reverse shows the chef, the hunting party and the ice-skating party.

Early 20th century/English

Right

Zoetrope. A circular metal drum with base but no top which pivots on a stand; the drum is pierced with vertical slots 2½in apart. The coloured paper strips are placed inside the drum with a picture below each slot and the base picture on the bottom of the drum. Each picture consists of slightly differently positioned drawings in sequence which give the illusion of movement when viewed through the slots whilst the drum is rotated. There were dozens of picture strips available, some with American interest such as the baseball player.

c 1860/Size: drum 11¾in diameter, 8¼in high; picture strip 36½ x 3½in

Peep-shows were not always static. In 1851 portable telescopes were hawked through London streets and cost 'a penny a peep'. Peep-showmen travelled the country districts, murders and battles being the most popular subjects. In hard times empty bottles were used for money and, as the showman remarked: 'Often two wants to see for one large bottle – the children is dreadful for cheapening things down'!

Another type of peep-show was the small carved bone or ivory model of an umbrella or parasol frequently sold as a souvenir of the Great Exhibition, or as a memento of the popular holiday resorts of Victorian England. These hollow parasols with removable stopper were really needle-cases and, like the many other peep-show souvenirs, were made in France. Through the minute lens at the handle end could be seen a series of views or buildings photographed on a microscopic scale. These peep-shows are still fairly readily available for collectors today and are usually 4½in high with a viewing aperture of ⅛in. An example of this size could have six pictures and six captions grouped round a central heading. Similar but slightly larger examples show as many as fourteen views with captions.

Thaumatrope
The thaumatrope (c 1826) was a simple toy which employed the eye's persistence of vision to give the effect of movement. It consisted of complementary inverted objects upon either side of a rotating disc operated by hand-twisting of a string. The tightly wound string and the release of tension gave the impression of the two objects uniting; for example, a soldier standing at attention on one side of the disc and an empty inverted sentry-box upon the other became, when the string was twisted, a small vignette of the soldier standing inside the box. There were endless variations of pairs of objects. Many optical toys rely on the principle of persistence of vision, some also using mirrors to heighten the effect, eg the praxinoscope. The phenakistoscope of the 1830s was an early device consisting of different sized discs, some hand coloured, which could be spun on a wooden handle.

Alternating picture toy
An amusing item, of which there are Victorian and Edwardian examples, is the hand-held alternating picture toy – sets of coloured pictures on card, held by cotton tapes which allow the pictures to fall in sequence and thus make different scenes.

Zoetrope, or 'Wheel of Life'
This toy was popular in the later Victorian era and, luckily for collectors, it is still possible to find examples for sale. Some models are more expensive than others, but more important than finding an elaborate machine is the condition of the collection of picture strips that went with it; better still if one can find a specimen with the dozen or so base pictures still in place.

Experiments and discoveries in the field of optical entertainment were going on long before Victoria's time, but it was undoubtedly the Great Exhibition of 1851 which focussed attention on the progress of technology. It is true to say that approximately the last three-quarters of the nineteenth century, from about 1826 to 1900, saw the introduction of the greatest number of optical novelties.

Throughout this period in Europe and America panoramic toys and various 'scopes' and 'tropes' followed each other in rapid succession, each proclaimed as the latest scientific invention. Progressively, the adult discovery became the nursery toy, first rare and then popular. All but the cheaper adaptations maintained a fair degree of craftsmanship, probably because they were made not only for children but for family entertainment. In the collecting world, this is where optical toys merge into optical antiques.

Polyorama panoptique
This device was a typical parlour-cum-nursery toy. It achieved the seemingly complex task of turning night into day and one scene into another, yet it was simple to operate and delighted adults and children alike.

Optical toys as teaching toys
It was apparent that optical toys could teach as well as amuse. Astronomy, for instance, was taught by means of slides and films showing the heavenly bodies in orbit. Not only did these toys display educative material, they also demonstrated the principles which optical research had established, thus achieving a dual purpose, a fact greatly appreciated by parents to whom instruction of the young mind was a strict priority.

Stereoscope
Travel was welcomed and enjoyed by the Victorians. The coming of the railway meant the easy transport of families and servants and established the heyday of the English seaside resort.

Since holidays abroad were not yet popular and cheap, people were really interested to view special cards showing, perhaps, the majesty of Conway Castle or the delights of donkey-riding on Ramsgate sands. This they did with the instrument called the stereoscope. There were large drawing-room models mounted in cabinets and smaller hand-held ones for the cheaper market. The cards to fit into the machine consisted of two adjacent but fractionally different pictures of the same object or scene. When viewed through the pair of lenses in the eyepiece, the two merged into one and gave the impression of depth and distance.

It should be possible for most collectors to find a stereoscope and set of cards.

Magic lanterns
The magic lantern, which had its origin in the seventeenth century, reached the height of its popularity in the nineteenth and was one of the best-loved Victorian toys (by parents as well as children). Its manufacture continued well into the twentieth century, with improvements of parts and accessories. Many of these boxed lanterns have attractive coloured labels with a picture of children both giving and enjoying the show and bearing the words 'Lanterna Magica – Made in Germany'.

It is certainly one of the best examples of an optical toy for the collector to seek and not too difficult to acquire since it was made in different sizes and there were many variations.

The range of slides – glass, plain and coloured photographic, lithographic etc – was comprehensive, including comic tale,

Below

Kaleidoscopic colour top (at left), consisting of a boxed collection of coloured card discs, divided and subdivided into green, yellow, blue etc, together with pierced black discs of intricate design. All parts fitted on to a string-operated top, giving a fine kaleidoscope of colour when spun. There are two labels on the box lid:

1.   Kaleidoscopic
             Colour Top
Invented and patented by John Gorham
2.   Wm. Ladd
            Optician
Manufacturer of Microscopes
Philosophical & Mathematical Instruments
31, Chancery Lane, London.

c 1858/60/Size: 5½in diameter, 4½in spindle
A manufacturer's or trade label on any item adds to its value.

At right, a stereoscope; a hand-held example. The correct focus for viewing the card was achieved by lengthening or shortening the distance of the card from the eyepiece. The sepia-toned stereoscopic photographs of the 1850s and 60s were commercially produced, but by the 1890s the amateur was able to buy a stereocamera and produce his own stereoviews.

Mid-19th century/English/Mounted cards: 7 x 3½in; stereoscope: 13in long

Above

Polyorama panoptique. A toy which enabled the viewer to see two different aspects of what appeared to be one picture. The amount of light entering the box could be varied by raising or lowering the top opening and the front flap, thus allowing a greater degree of light for exterior and day-time scenes, or a dim light for interior or night-time scenes.

eg A slide of Constantinople and Balaclava showing a peaceful day-time scene of Constantinople with river and craft in the foreground (top fully opened and front flap angled).

also A stirring scene of soldiers before battle, grouped round their glowing camp fires (top closed and front flap fully opened).

A slide of St Paul's, London, showing a day-time scene of the cathedral with the old houses and the river in the foreground (top fully opened and front flap angled).

also A clear but sombre view of the vaulted interior, showing details of stonework and light entering from the high glass windows (top closed and front flap fully opened).
The paper slides for this apparatus were cunningly contrived, delicately hand coloured and pierced appropriately for starlight, moonlight, firelight and gunfire! There were twelve such slides for the popular table model.

Mid-19th century/French/Box: 9in x 4¾in

nursery tales, natural history and that essential final picture – 'Good night!'

There is a bonus in the study of the titles for the lithographed films, as they give a wonderful social commentary. Here are seven from a manufacturer's list of fifty-four:

'Steerable airship flying'
'Girl playing Diabolo'
'Comical street cleaner'
'Coon Dance'
'In the Air (Bleriot)'
'Balloon ascent at Rheims'
'A journey in an Airship.'

After 1914, it was the new 'projecting lanterns' from America which, together with powerful illumination, made possible the reproduction of coloured cards, magazine pages etc, and meant that the entertainment was no longer limited to the use of transparent glass slides.

Kaleidoscope

The kaleidoscope was patented by Sir David Brewster in 1817, but was possibly oriental in origin. It was, basically, a special arrangement of mirrors within a tube which, upon rotation, enabled coloured pieces of glass to be seen in an infinite variety of patterns and could be used by designers studying the effects of symmetrical patterns. From Sir David's invention developed all sorts of kaleidoscopic toys.

Nowadays the same principle is employed in cheap cardboard tubes with coloured 'silver' paper fragments replacing the coloured glass.

It is interesting to note that many of these old optical inventions were sold at opticians' shops rather than at toyshops – an indication that craftsmanship was highly valued.

Photography inevitably played an ever-increasing role in optical novelties, particularly when it became possible to shorten the time allowed for each exposure and thus present a sequence of photographs of the same object taken in quick succession, and with only minimal difference in the actual positioning of the object or action. This link in the chain of development is admirably illustrated by the kinora.

Some of the constructional optical toys – the 'do it yourself' items – were difficult to make, but children were encouraged to make their own amusements and the luckier ones often had a room of their own or a nursery where half-finished projects could be safely left until the next day.

Illustrated opposite is the 'Construments 100 Outfit – Every Boy & Girl a Scientist'. All of the items described really could be made from the parts supplied. The manufacturer's instruction book of thirty-six closely printed pages with diagrams gave details for making no less than eighty-one models! There was even a paragraph on how to collect finger prints and enlarge them – having first made your own photo-copier and enlarger!

Research, together with the development of photographic techniques, advanced optical science at a tremendous rate. Even a few examples of optical toys will enable the collector to look beyond the frontier of the tangible into a magical world of shadows, of changing shapes, textures and colours, of faces and places fixed upon glass and celluloid.

From the early peep-shows and the many inventions leading to the first films has come much of the knowledge culminating in our sophisticated television. Each step along the way must have been a wonder and a triumph.

At left, combination cinematograph and magic lantern, constructed of black japanned tin with back opening for paraffin lamp. Either cellofilms or glass slides could be used; included in the outfit was an instruction leaflet in six languages.

Early 20th century / German / Size: height with chimney 12in, base 7½ x 4 in, slides 4 x 1in, black lithographed films 22in long consisting of 30 pictures
At right, an earlier model, also of black japanned tin, with candle illumination. It took larger coloured transfer printed slides.

c 1866 / German / 7¾ x 2¾ in

Foreground, chromotrope slide. This could be used as an accessory for the magic lantern. Framed in wood and turned by a handle at the side, a combination of coloured designs could be achieved by a revolving process (giving much the same effect as the kaleidoscope). This slide carries the handwritten inscription: 'Gogerty Optician 72 Fleet St'.

c 1907 / Length: 7 x 4in

A somewhat similar item was the 'comic slipping slide' which had amusing little figures appearing to skip, dance etc (and some of much broader humour for showing when the children had been despatched to bed!).

Above

At right, a kinora. This apparatus was advertised as an achievement in animated photography. It had a powerful magnifying glass, but the picture reels were the secret of its success – these were easily changed, and consisted of a circular-bound sequence of printed photographs which were moved on in rapid succession by turning the handle, giving the effect of life-like movement. Most kinora machines were hand operated, but one could buy a clockwork-automated sequence viewer and some had three viewing lenses. The reels showed many different subjects – the zoo, the circus, the horse-race etc. The principle of this toy is still used today in the manufacture of the cheap, paper cartoon booklets which children flip quickly between their fingers.

Early 20th century/American/Height: 8in

A kaleidoscope (at left) of painted brass mounted on a wooden stand. The colours of the interior patterns are soft and muted by today's standards.

Mid-19th century/English/Height: 12in

Right

A magic lantern with circular brass burner compartment, funnel and scroll supports to the lens-tube. There are six revolving slides, three educative – human races, portraits and geology – and three with narrative scenes showing Little Red Riding Hood, Puss-in-Boots and Robinson Crusoe, the latter so designed in sequence that the story evolved as the slide turned. The trade-mark medallion is marked E.P. for Ernst Planck.

c late 19th century/German/Height: 12in

Above

Construments 100 outfit, 'The Hobby of Ten Thousand Thrills'.

A scientific outfit for a child consisting of various interchangeable parts – screws, lenses, etc – contained in a cardboard cabinet with drawers, from which could be made: signalling lamps, torches, microscopes, shadowgraphs, pinhole cameras, photo-copiers, photo-printers, kaleidoscopes, magic lanterns, watch projectors, reflectoscopes, epidiascopes etc.

A quote from the manufacturer's advertisement gives a breathtaking idea of what the toy was intended to achieve: 'Infinite Variety – Fascinating Novelty – Spectacular Effects – Exploration of the Unknown – Endless Entertainment – Valuable Instruction – Scientific Marvels' etc. It was also claimed that the toy would 'stimulate research, initiative, education, ingenuity and inventiveness'. (All this for 37s 6d plus 1s extra for the battery!)

First quarter of 20th century/English

Mirth, Magic
and Mystery

Puppets

Eastern countries were renowned for their shadow puppets, still used and loved today. The Javanese shadow puppets have been known for almost 1000 years and many of the dramas portrayed have their origins in the great Indian epics. Attendance at the plays was very much a family affair and could last all night with the whole community enjoying the play and the social gathering.

People of medieval England also enjoyed puppet plays; these were chiefly of religious origin and both methods of animation were used – the glove or hand puppets (operated from below) and the string variety (operated from above). Early puppets, although watched by adults, were also sold as toys for children. Contemporary engravings showed puppet-sellers, and Hogarth's print of 'Southwark Fair' illustrated dancing dolls. Punch, although accepted as thoroughly English, was of Italian origin and by the early eighteenth century he and his nagging wife Judy had assumed the physical features we know today. The old puppet heads were made of carved and painted wood or leather and later of papier mâché and composition. When joints were necessary, they were made as flexible as possible.

Few people realise that ventriloquism is an ancient art, once practised by priests and prophets of early civilisations. It means literally to 'speak from the stomach' and the early exponents were called 'belly prophets'! The ventriloquist is really a voice illusionist and the dummies are constructed so that unseen manipulation of eyes and limbs will deceive the audience.

In some dummies it is possible to raise the front portion of the wig so that, in moments of surprise or horror, the figure is actually seen to have a 'hair-raising' experience.

The ventriloquist's doll and the modern puppets of stage, screen and television are usually presented by adults for the enjoyment of children, but it is perhaps only in modern England that puppet plays are considered a juvenile entertainment. In many countries puppet dramas are part of the adult experience, keeping alive the old traditions and also holding a mirror to contemporary life. However, the art of puppetry was something children quickly learned from the grown-up world. They could use toy puppets, or they could model the heads of papier mâché and design and make the costumes, so that the complete drama was a group project. If possible, a toy collection should show shadow, string and glove puppets.

Toy Theatres

It was inevitable that the theatre, beloved of the adult world, should be reproduced as a toy. Its creative potential was enormous – would-be actors and stage managers could light the scene, speak the script, colour the scenery, move the characters, make the music and ring down the curtain. It all took a long time, but that was part of the fun. In England there were many publishers of juvenile drama and the collector should keep in mind the names of West, Green, Skelt, Redington and Pollock, the sheets priced at one penny plain and twopence coloured.

Conjurors

In a book about toys it would be pedantic to distinguish between sleight-of-hand and illusion. Conjuring in its widest interpretation was practised by the ancient Egyptians and in those early times religious images were given 'life' by hidden manipulation of limbs and eyes. Throughout the ages man has sought to mystify the uninitiated.

In more recent times the list of conjurors and magicians must include Robert Houdin (1805-1871) and his Theatre of Magic in Paris, the English family of Maskelyne at St Georges Hall, London, and that great escape artist of this century – Houdini. Once upon a time, a tall hat, cloak, beard and wand were considered the proper garb for a dispenser of magic. Not for the old wizards were the dress clothes and polished manner of today. This change must have originated when magic lost its element of witchcraft and entered the Victorian parlour and the popular entertainment halls.

Whilst doll-play was associated with girls, magic was a male preserve. Generations of boys have tried their hand (and patience) at perfecting simple tricks in an effort to impress their friends. In the days before one counter in a store had replaced the toyshop proper, as is now the case, a few specialist toyshops were noted for their stock of

Above

At left, a pink-faced puppet used for the 'Wayang Kulit' (kulit means skin). In these shadow plays, the profile figures were attached to sticks and the screen was lit from behind to cast a shadow. Making these flat skin puppets was a folk art – skilled artists prepared and cut the hides according to traditional patterns and their decoration and colouration had specific meaning. The village audiences could, and did, behave informally, but the atmosphere was entirely spiritual.

At right, a puppet for the 'Wayang Golek'. It is a half figure of carved and decorated wood, with gold and scarlet ornamentation. The upper body is shaped and wears a sarong; the head is turned by a central pole which also supports the silhouette.

c 1870 / Javanese / Height: hide puppet 25½ in; wooden puppet 22½ in

Right

A group of Punch and Judy glove puppets. The heads are of painted wood with turned wooden arms and legs, and the puppets are worked by three fingers of one hand operating inside the loose dresses.

c 1880 / German / Height: 15½ in

Children found the glove puppets easier to manage than the string puppets or marionettes.

Above

A Pollock toy theatre of an early design showing the metal slides for moving the characters.

c 1860–70 / English / Size: 23½ in high x 21 in wide

magic, conjuring and toy theatre equipment. Thus, in the mid-nineteenth century, the young stage enthusiast could buy all the tinted foils and silks needed to ornament the printed portraits of stage celebrities. These were assembled at home and stuck onto the portraits. Although the colours were sometimes garish, the finished decoration gave vivid reality to the otherwise rather lifeless prints.

A rare 1884 *Catalogue of Conjuring Apparatus* gives so many examples of magical novelties that one could assume this to be the heyday of tricks and surprises. No less than 175 items could be acquired for only one shilling. 'The Great Davenport Cabinet' cost five shillings and for two guineas you could buy 'The Juggler's Cabinet of Legerdemain' which was described as 'surpassing the Enchantments of the Eastern Wizards'. The 'Magician's Box' or 'Cabinet of Tricks' has altered very little – in fact the earlier examples seem the more adventurous. In 1884 you could also buy a 'Diabolical Box containing sixteen articles – including sheet lightning, silver fire, Pharoah's serpent, Japanese fire, stars and limelight', all for one shilling.

To save up one's pocket money and buy a shilling trick was one thing. It was quite another to receive a gift of a whole cabinet of tricks. These cabinets, together with the chemistry sets, must have been the Victorian's answer to the question 'What shall we get him for Christmas?'

Jokes and tricks within the pocket money range included 'The Wonderful Nose Knife' (cutting off a person's nose), 'The Great Blood Writing Trick' (names appeared written in blood on the performer's arm) and 'The Great Nose and Twine Trick' (the performer first bores a hole through the gentleman's nose with a bradawl – 'Very Laughable'). It must have been a relief to peer at one's tortured figure in the popular 'Distorting Mirror'.

Above
A ventriloquist's dummy with hollow composition body, legs and hands. A rod moves the papier mache head and the string-operated mouth and eyes can be moved at the same time. The loose-hanging arms and legs can assume any position, whilst the dummy sits firmly on an entirely flat base. Dressed in striped trousers, black coat and white shirt.

c 1910/English/Height: 35in

Above
A cabinet of conjuring tricks with instructions and equipment for performing fifteen tricks.

c 1930s/English

Right
A perforated picture cut from an old document. The shadow of this cut-out portrait of Cupid could be projected on to a wall by a light held at the proper distance and angle.

c 1840/English

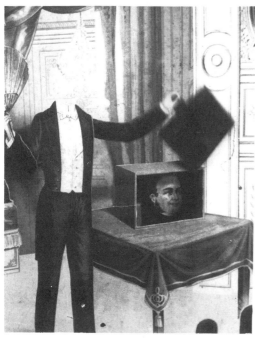

Above

A cut-out cardboard scene of a conjuring entertainment with clockwork movement. The conjuror, when wound up and in motion, performs the trick of seeming to become headless – whilst the head appears in a box on the table. A fan moves in front of the face whilst this spectacle is enacted! Meanwhile one person in the gallery applauds and another member of the audience nods his head in appreciation.

c 1890/English/Size: 20 x 28½ in framed

Ghosts and goblins. The peculiarities of the human eye were cleverly exploited by J. H. Brown in 1863. He wrote a book called *Spectropia or Surprising Spectral Illusions showing Ghosts Everywhere And of Any Colour*! The illusions were founded on the persistency of impressions and the production of complementary colours on the retina. The illustrations were painted in complementary colours and had a small central dot on which to focus the eyes and concentrate the gaze. Thus a black-hooded monk had to be stared at for twenty-five seconds and the gaze then quickly transferred to wall or ceiling. Astonishingly, a phantom-like replica appeared and then slowly faded. Similarly, Mr. Punch and dog Toby, painted in red and blue, appeared as green and yellow spectres. The ghostly subjects included a long, fleshless hand, angels floating on clouds and a witch on a broomstick! The effects were startling and produced a thrill of fascinated horror – one really had seen a ghost!

Indoor Games, Constructional Toys and Pastimes

In many lands and from ancient times, mankind has whiled away his time (and sometimes his fortune) by pitting his wits at contests of chance or skill. The majority of board and all gambling games were intended for adults, but chess, dominoes, draughts, halma, ludo, bezique, solitaire and many others were also played by children and some were simplified or adapted to teach as well as amuse. Children, of course, did not win or lose money, but used cowrie shells or counters.

The early board games were often race games too, and involved forfeits or turn of position. The famous 'Royal Game of Goose' (c 1725) was the forerunner of many amusing and instructional spiral games from which 'Snakes and Ladders' and a host of other dice and counter games have evolved. The Victorian version of 'Snakes and Ladders' taught typically moral lessons. The player went up the labelled ladders from Industry to Prosperity, from Punctuality to Advancement – and down the marked snakes from Pride to a Fall, Bad Temper to Murder and Stealing to Prison!

Cards were originally a grown-up pastime or gambling device, whereas children's card games were for amusement only. There were, of course, some card games which children could play using simple rules and the conventional pack. Later on, manufacturers produced illustrated packs especially for children, such as Happy Families, Animal Grab, Snap, etc.

In the days before radio and television, when evenings were long and difficulties of travel kept children at home, games were a great part of family life. Parents intended that their children should absorb some knowledge whilst they played. The early map-makers first published dissected puzzles in the eighteenth century and, although many of them were maps there were others with a moral intent and all were designed to educate through play. The invention of the jigsaw enabled more intricate puzzles to be cut and as the century progressed and parental attitudes altered and relaxed, so did the subject matter of the puzzles. Examples teaching history, geography and religion were still made, but amusing and entertaining puzzles also appeared. At last a child could enjoy his

Right
Background, the board of a race game showing very early aeroplanes. It must have been an imaginary journey, as none of the 'planes depicted could possibly have flown to Sydney or Johannesburg!

c 1912/English

Centre, 'Golliwogg' card game. This was based on the books by Florence and Bertha Upton from which the drawings were reproduced. Centre foreground, 'Happy Families' card game. Described as 'A New and Most Diverting Game for Juveniles'; the earlier packs consisted of forty-four cards with square corners and included such amusing family names as Bun the Baker, Bones the Butcher, Grits the Grocer etc. The later editions added Mug the Milkman and the cards had rounded corners. By John Jaques & Son Ltd, London; this firm produced many popular card games for children.

Late 19th century

At right, table croquet. Part of a boxed set containing polished mallets, painted balls and metal hoops. The field of play was marked by a webbing boundary.

Early 20th century/English/Size: mallets 9½in

Right foreground, spellicans – the game was to disengage each spellican from the pile without touching or moving another. Many children played the same game using spent matches.

c Victorian/English/Size: bone spellicans 4in long

'Attracto or Catch 'em', a fishing game consisting of tiny metal fish which were caught by means of a magnet attached to a wooden rod.

Early 20th century/English
Right
'Jiggle Joggle' the frog race game; large green card frogs were raced the length of the room by means of cords which were slackened or pulled by the player holding the other end of the cord. A special outdoor edition was supplied for use 'on the lawn in summer'.

Early 20th century/English/Size: frogs 13in

At right, 'Aunt Sally'; a toy version similar to the adult game played at fairs and fêtes. The rings had to be skilfully thrown to lodge on to the pipe. Here, the face and pipe are of painted wood; in the adult game, a clay pipe would have been used.

English/Height: 20in

Below left, 'Box Ball'; a game of suspended skittles, each in a separate gate and numbered so that the highest scorer was the winner. The skill was in the strength with which the ball was rolled through the gates – too hard and the swinging skittle knocked it out again.

Early 20th century/American/Size: 9 x 5½ x 3in

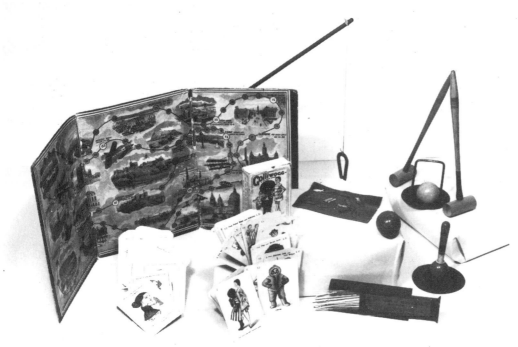

Above
A boxed set of blocks, making six different pictures.

c 1900/English/Size of completed puzzle: 10¾ x 15¾in

Above
'My Birthday Presents: Indestructible Double Puzzle', ascribed to the firm of J. W. Barfoot (1860s). One side shows children playing with a variety of toys and the reverse illustrates the story of Little Red Riding Hood.

c 1868 (there is a handwritten birthday inscription on the back dated 1868)/English/Size: 12 x 9in

Above
An oak constructional toy; each wall of the house has strong wires running from top to bottom on which are threaded thirty-two courses of small wooden blocks of different sizes.

c 1887 (the date is carved on the front)/English/Size: platform 13 x 16in; house 14 x 8½ x 10½in

Above
'The Little Connoisseur of Wood'. A construction set containing shaped, polished and stained blocks.

c 1900/German/Size boxed: 18 x 15in

playtime without having a multitude of facts stuffed into his head at the same time. The boxes containing the puzzles are worth studying and help the collector to date the puzzle – the stronger and more elegant the box, the earlier the puzzle. Later examples were made with cheaper wood.

The alphabet and basic spelling were also taught through play. Blocks had letters pasted on to the sides and various word games appeared. Quick reactions were encouraged by pairing pictures of familiar objects – a pictorial form of Lotto – and memories were trained through 'Kim's game' – looking at small items on a tray and then listing them from memory.

By contrast, later Victorian and Edwardian children's games, particularly those in which the whole family could join, were often small-scale versions of adult games and sports, such as skittles, indoor bowls, table croquet etc. All children like to win, so competitive family games enabled the parents to encourage sportsmanship and the loser had to accept defeat gracefully or, at least, in silence!

The game of ninepins preceded skittles and these novelty sets were attractively presented: 9 kittens in a gilded basket, 9 vegetables in a cabbage, 9 jockeys in a jockey's head, the trunk of a tree containing 9 rabbits and (for the grown-ups) a large basket containing 9 bottles of champagne!

Constructional toys

Clay mixed with water and dried in the sun must have been one of the oldest modelling materials. And cooks, ancient and modern, have contributed trimmings from bread or pastry dough to make the inedible, grubby and fantastical creations of the youngest modeller. Wax, too, was used extensively, but more as an artist's medium than a child's toy.

In 1897 William Harbutt invented his famous modelling material Plasticine, which generations of children have used and loved (the firm sounded the true patriotic note in 1915 with its slogan: 'No more German toys for us – we can make fings for ourselves wif Plasticine'!).

Children making sand castles and mud-and-water huts are improvising constructional toys. Manufacturers merely supplied

the ready-made components to facilitate this sort of play, and it is thus difficult to put such toys into a separate category. Many could be described as educational toys, some were also paper toys (Micromodels) and one could say that the early matchwood boxes filled with small wooden models of houses, churches, farms and so on became constructional toys when they were aligned and set out as villages. However, the box of plain wooden blocks which an imaginative child could build up and balance at will was a basic constructional toy which has survived the centuries.

From plain or painted wood it was an obvious step to manufacture blocks with parts of pictures pasted onto each of the six sides, so that complete pictures could be assembled by placing the blocks in the correct position. The scenes were usually of religious interest, or nursery objects, farm animals, etc. One suspects that in stricter households, making up the religious pictures was one of the few games allowed on Sundays.

Children first build copies of the things they see around them, so the toymakers produced building sets which included a few basic shapes – doors, arches, windows, pitched roofs etc. Then came the refinement of pieces made of real stone, coloured in neutral shades, soft pinks and blues. These boxed sets came in various sizes and prices. The cheaper kind had merely the outlines of windows and doors stamped on to the blocks, whilst the finer sets contained blocks especially shaped to construct miniature buildings. Perhaps they were intended to teach the rudiments of architecture and certainly the result looked like a real building with the arches, pillars, pediments etc, all reproduced to scale.

Boxed sets of Victorian building bricks sometimes had delightful names on the box lids. Children were not just building houses, they were constructing the 'Principal Edifices of Europe' or 'Country Seats'. The child was not merely playing with bricks, he was 'A Little Connoisseur of Wood'.

Amongst the makers of stone building sets, firstly Richter (Germany) and, later, Lott (England) were perhaps two of the best known. Richter's stone 'Anchor Blocks' and Lott's 'Bricks' and 'Tudor Blocks' could be made up into realistic architectural models.

If Richter's 'Anchor Bricks' and Lott's 'Stone Bricks' were the toys of the budding architect and builder, 'Meccano' was certainly the toy of the young engineer. The components of all three were made to scale – an important fact in the education of aspiring professionals.

'Meccano', invented by Frank Hornby and the original system first patented in 1901, was one of the best loved constructional toys. It was especially good because it could be 'built up' – the 00 set (first set) for the young child could be augmented until the final sets were needed by the older boy to make the 'Meccano Super Models'. These were truly challenging and required special instruction leaflets – a three engine biplane, traction engine (driven by a 6-volt motor), motor cycle and sidecar, Baltic tank locomotive, motor chassis with gear box, clutch, differential, internal expanding brakes etc. To assist the real engineering concept, Meccano marketed power units – electric motors, transformers, steam engines and clockwork motors. Collectors should note that the early outfits were uncoloured; later sets were coloured.

Toy collectors owe much to the name of Hornby – the construction toy, the clockwork trains and the *Meccano Magazine* which dealt not only with hobbies, travel and the latest inventions, but also included advertisements for the things boys love – chemistry sets, stamps, matchbox labels, joke pages, competitions and air pistols!

Constructional toys could be made up using screws, clips, pegs, wires and in many other ingenious ways, but interlocking, grooved and interchangeable pieces comprised a novel method of assembly. Crandall of America made some of the finest toys using this idea (c last quarter of the nineteenth century). His 'School', 'Menagerie' and 'Acrobats' were three of the most famous examples and any collector obtaining one of these has a true 'find'.

Amongst the post popular constructional toys of the 1950s were Micromodels, cut-out cards which could be made into true scale models and were advertised as 'miniature replicas of interesting and beautiful Mechanical, Architectural, Industrial and

Above
A 'Meccano Accessory Outfit'. The sets were numbered, beginning at 00 and were converted by adding an accessory outfit (A). Thus a no 0A set converted a no 0 set into a no 1 set. The instruction manuals were clearly produced, giving the illustration and parts required for each model.

Early 20th century/English

Above
Part of a collection of ten cut-out cards printed in colour and depicting a battleship, field guns, army aeroplane, armoured train, Red Cross motor ambulance, lighthouse, fort, armoured motor cycle, soldiers and national flags. Published by Raphael Tuck & Sons Ltd.

c 1915-1920/English/Size: 13½ x 10in

Above
Two from a set of ninepins fashioned as kittens with the King or Kingpin wearing scarlet jacket and crown. The nine velvet kittens have realistic markings, neck ribbons and bells and are mounted on satinwood bases.

c 1884/English/Height: 8½in

Left
A selection of Micromodels showing historic buildings, fully-rigged sailing ship and locomotive.

c 1950s/English/Various sizes, cards 5 x 3½in

Maritime subjects ... printed on card to form accurate three-dimensional volumetric models'. Their construction needed care and much patience, but to the devoted model maker who wished to make a miniature museum of his own, they were one of the most satisfying constructional toys ever invented.

Any toy which can be taken apart, reconstructed or, better still, made up into something else, stimulates a child's creative imagination as no finished or completed toy can ever do. Handwork, too, is most satisfying even though the beginner has to use instructions and patterns. Bead, metal and poker-work were hobbies children loved and from them they learned the first principles of design. Boys with fret-saws made family presents, usually letter- or pipe-racks for father, and little girls busied themselves making dolls' clothes with their toy sewing machines.

The American invention of the sewing machine which made the name 'Singer' a household word was copied for children. The toy machines were, of course, extremely simple, the turning handle merely raising and lowering the needle. Cheaper models were of tin, the more solid examples of cast iron, but most could really 'sew', often using a simple chain stitch.

Many Victorian games have survived because they were packed well. Bricks, blocks, puzzles and building sets had their own strongly made wooden boxes. Today's toys are attractively presented from the buyer's point of view, but once the transparent covering has been ripped off in order to get at the toy, there is then no permanent container in which to keep and preserve it.

Sounds and Celebrations

Since pagan times mankind has celebrated the seasons of the year, and later civilisations have honoured Saints' days and festivals. The Nativity scene, with crèche figures, was loved by grown-up and child alike and devotional toys including candlesticks, bells and even musical toy organs were popular in Catholic countries in the nineteenth century.

Easter, a time of great religious significance, is also a Spring festival. The egg has long been a symbol of fertility and through the centuries the Easter egg has come to represent this season of rebirth. Eggs were decorated and painted with natural dyes, seasonal dishes of herbs cooked, special foods prepared and specific rites observed.

Christenings, birthdays, marriages and other important personal occasions were also marked by established rites. The Japanese doll festival is famous for its recognition of the Girls' Festival and the Boys' Festival – both with strong family and

Sound toys: the cow with neck movement moos and has a compartment at the back which can be filled and the cow then 'milked'. The feathered cock crows realistically when the front lever is depressed.

Victorian/English/Sizes: cow 12½in long; cock 12in high

Centre, a toy gramophone in painted tin-plate case with conical horn attaching to soundbox.

Early 20th century/German (Bing 'pigmyphone')/Size: 6¼ x 6¼in

At left, a speaking picture book, described as 'imitating the cries of animals. An Amusement for the little ones' eyes and ears'. The instructions were: 'Pull the cords sharply and the animals will speak for themselves'. There are eight imitations – cock, donkey, goat, duck, sheep, cat, cow and horse, with illustrations and accompanying verses.

Victorian/Size: 12 x 9½ x 2in

At right, metal drum with sticks and tin violin. Date and origin unknown, but both are typical nursery toys.

ancestral ties. In many lands the customs which have developed from particular ceremonies included the presentation of gifts, many of which were toys.

Traditional play is ritualistic, with rules and forms handed down from generation to generation. Different localities have variations of many games, but the theme is the same. The skipping rhymes and hopping patterns may differ slightly but are instantly recognised.

Sound delights a child almost as much as visual appeal. Rattles in infancy were followed by whistles, drums, tambourines, mouth-organs, squeaking and musical toys. Noise combined with splendour and surprise was even better, and fireworks had both. In the western world of the seventeenth century however, only the military fireworks could help the people to celebrate times of national rejoicing. Modern firework displays did not really begin until the early nineteenth century, though manufacturers were quick to produce small items for children.

Taste was important too, but, for obvious reasons, not many tasting-toys survived. Some of the finest were made in eighteenth-century Germany, when gum tragacanth and other ingredients were used. These little toys were excellently designed and sometimes contained a motto. Recorded in print, rhyme or wooden mould were the bread dolls of medieval England and the gilt ginger-bread men of fairground and market stall. Today we remember the sugar mice with string tails, edible Easter eggs, jelly babies and those exciting chocolate cigars and cigarettes which were 'puffed' defiantly in front of parents.

Spring and harvest toys. The eggs, cardboard (left) and wooden (right), are both made in two halves and would have contained a gift. Other 'egg' toys were the nesting eggs which fitted one inside the other (very much like the Russian nesting dolls) and the wooden eggs which enclosed miniature peg wooden dolls of less than ¼in – 'the smallest dolls in the world'. Centre, the corn dolly – a modern interpretation of a traditional design, one of many designs reputed to have originated as symbolic offerings to the gods for a fruitful harvest. Straw shapes were also made as Christmas decorations in northern Europe. ('Dolly' does not mean doll-shaped).

English/Height: 14in

Below, a cardboard reproduction of a 'Hot Cross Bun', which would have been filled with chocolates. The opening is in the base where a tab pulls up the flap to reveal the gift inside.

Early 20th century/English (label TOM SMITH).

Christmas toys, all early 20th century. At left, a model of Father Christmas with a hollow carton body to be filled with sweets.

English/Height: 7½in

Centre, a wax fairy doll dressed in silk net for the Christmas tree. It has inserted hair, painted features and is marked with the original price – 10s.

English/Height: 11in

At right, a doll associated with the continental Christmas – the 'Knave Rupprecht' doll, with bisque head and covered with white fur.

European/Height: 12in

Toys in Advertising

Until World War I, Germany was the chief supplier of advertising toys and although these were early days for this type of marketing, there was a good profit to be made, since items were ordered not in dozens, but often by the million. Such things as cardboard and paper novelties, booklets, flat wooden puzzles, pocket knives, pencil cases and cheap metal items were bought by specialist buyers for resale to commercial firms seeking to promote their sales. After 1918 British manufacturers supplied similar novelties – many of a type known to the trade as 'Birmingham goods' – but America was eventually to take the lead in this particular field of toy production.

The inclusion of a gift for the child in the product itself, or in the packaging of the product bought by the mother is not a new idea. In 1885, Wilson's American baby biscuits of Philadelphia issued a twenty-page booklet entitled 'Great Fun For The Little Ones'. Each page had black and white drawings showing how to make hand-shadows on the wall, plus instructions for playing a simple game and a few short sentences on the excellence of the biscuits.

The Edwardian coloured booklets of Colman's included 'Parlour Magic', 'Rhymes and Tunes' and the story of 'The Foolish Little Frog' with the customary caution in the last two verses:

A selection of advertising toys: the Wilson's booklet (baby biscuits), Colman's booklets (mustard, starch and Robinson's patent groats); decorated egg-cup ('A Present from Clifton'); Cadbury's reward card (cocoa – given as a reward for Sunday School attendance). 'Pip, Squeak and Wilfred' cup (*Daily Mirror* newspaper).

'And the moral for you
Is, don't say "Pooh"
Whatever your "din-din" be.
To the silly little sinner
Who hasn't had his dinner
It's a long, long time till tea!'

Children's card games were another cheap form of advertising. Cow & Gate, makers of baby foods, issued a set of comical cards similar to 'Happy Families' and each card advertised the firm together with the slogan 'The Food the Quads Thrived On'. Alfred Bird & Sons Ltd (now General Foods Ltd) also used the game of 'Happy Families' to launch their product of 'Jelly-de-Luxe'. Small-scale cards were given away inside each packet and the company gave a normal-sized pack in return for the collected set.

In his book *The History of the English Toy Theatre* George Speaight reports that, between the wars, a few firms put out toy theatres and plays as advertisements, with Caley's, Quaker·Oats and the London Un-

derground entering the toy theatre trade.

The more durable advertising toys were those made of metal or china with the advertiser's name or product lettered onto the actual toy. This was more expensive than the ephemeral give-away booklets, but also more successful, since once the contents had been consumed the toy remained for use as something else, thus keeping the advertiser's name in circulation for more than a lifetime – for example, Cadbury's milk churn (once filled with chocolates), and Huntley and Palmer's vending machine (once filled with biscuits).

This type of advertising material also included children's souvenir china, often with nursery motifs. Thus a bowl, plate or egg-cup bearing the name of a seaside town continued to advertise the resort where it was originally purchased. Similarly, the *Daily Mirror* china decorated with the 'Pip, Squeak and Wilfred' trio was a perpetual reminder of the paper.

Cadbury's ran a membership club called the C-Cubs (Cadbury Cubs) with its own

Above
'Betty Oxo'. A doll which was obtainable from Oxo Ltd, of London, in exchange for Oxo cube wrappers or the equivalent number of Oxo bottle metal caps. In the 1930s the same firm used other advertising toys – the Oxo football and cricket bat. In 1925 another doll was offered for the largest number of wrappers received, called 'Little Miss Oxo'. Dressed in pink velvet jacket and hat. Doll has stuffed fabric body with printed features; limbs covered in velvet, and metal-pinned to body. The woven label on the sole of the foot reads:

SPECIALLY MADE FOR
OXO LTD.
DEANS RAG BOOK CO.
LONDON

c 1936/English/Height: 16½in

Left
'Sunny Jim', a cut-out rag doll, lithographed on material, which was obtainable with 'Force' cereal tokens.

c 1909/Height: 16in

A model railway station carrying advertisements for Nestlé's Milk, Bovril and Oxo. The makers of model railway equipment and road vehicles charged advertising space on the toys which carried miniature replica advertisements. Model shops have long been nursery favourites and the makers of later examples seized the opportunity of slipping in a little advertising material so that many of the tiny packets, tins and bottles bore the name of the real manufacturer.

Cadbury's milk churn; painted tin with removable lid and slot for money.

c 1920/Height: 5½in

Huntley & Palmers biscuit vending machine.
Early 20th century/Height 9in

booklet, badge, password and annual. Belonging to a club was a sure way of maintaining interest in a company and junior membership of clubs, with specialised publications and badges, was frequently offered. The quality of the Meccano magazine was as admirable as the spirit of brotherhood which it advanced and, together with a world-wide subscription list, it must have been highly successful. A distinction should be drawn between toys used as incentives to buy and included with or obtainable from the manufacturers of the product, and those used in direct advertising, which actually included the advertiser's name (as on cigarette cards, miniature tins, packets, etc).

Packaging as toys

Representational biscuit tins and other metal containers were designed for visual impact. Popular at the end of the nineteenth century and marketed until 1937, many had a special appeal to children. Decorated tin imitations of handbags, cannon, miniature

Right
Window or counter display toy of a drinking bear automaton which sits on a painted tin log containing the driving batteries, with switch at the back. The bear pours 'Quality Pepsi-Cola' into a glass and drinks it, the liquid returning down through the arms back into the bottle.

c 1950/Japanese/Height: 10in

Far right
Following the elegant fashion dolls of the early nineteenth century, this 'naughty' wax lady of 100 years later shows the latest styles in lingerie and corsetry (note the anklet, garter and hair style).

c 1920/English/Height: 16½in

library books, kitchen ranges, gypsy vans, motorcars, ships and lighthouses all found their way into toy cupboards. They are collected today as toys and as examples of novelty packaging, now sadly replaced by cheap, disposable wrapping.

Trademarks as toys

In this type of advertising toy, one of the best known examples must be the Robertson's golliwog, used as a symbol since 1910. It has been, and still is, part of everyone's childhood to save the paper gollies and exchange them for a brooch or model. In 1946 a golly brooch could be redeemed for twelve golly labels and later a cricketer, a tennis player and a hockey player were added to the range and there have been golly footballers and musicians. The firm is still despatching thousands of pottery figures each week to children all over the world.

Cards

Perhaps the tobacco manufacturers hit upon one of the best ideas with their issues of cigarette cards. When cigarettes were sold in paper packs, rather than in thin cardboard packets, the card was slipped inside to keep the packet firm and save the contents from damage. Later, the name of the manufacturer was added, plus a picture in a numbered series of designs. These sets were of popular interest – film stars, sportsmen, service uniforms, wildlife etc, and millions of fathers must have been persuaded to purchase packet after packet in order to obtain the elusive missing number. Instantly a cheap form of advertising was allied to the collecting instinct and success was assured. Some manufacturers also thoughtfully provided albums or sheets in which to display the completed sets. Nowadays, cards of this type are found in tea and cereal packets.

Collectors may consider that cigarette cards cannot be classed as toys and yet they were very much part of a child's world. They were certainly in the forefront of advertising initiative directed towards the junior members of the family in order to bring 'buying-pressure' to bear upon the parents.

Display toys

With the coming of electricity, attractions included motivated toys and lighted displays of all kinds in shop windows.

Note for collectors

The list of toys used in advertising is extensive, and collecting them would be a fascinating side-line for the collector and is, as yet, under-researched. Many companies, both in Europe and America, advertised their products with small gifts, souvenirs and special offers. They were mostly cheap, inconsequential trifles – which will make it all the more challenging to discover them – but, correspondingly, the prices should be very reasonable.

Examples from a range of metal animals used by Cadbury's to promote cocoa sales. There were two issues: the first used well-known nursery characters – the hen (Mrs Henrietta Fussyfeathers) and the pig (Mr Pie Porker); the second included the old favourites and one or two more exotic animals, such as the penguin and the kangaroo.

c pre-1939/English/Height: about 1½in

Woven silk inserts depicting flowers. These are from a set of 60 in the Kensitas Flower series. The silk pictures could be 'framed' in a card folder on which was printed a few lines of appropriate verse, a short history of the flower and cultural notes for its successful cultivation.

c 1935/English/Height: 2 x 2¾in

Glass Toys

Glass, like paper and wax, would seem a most unlikely material for the toy-maker and it says much for the skill of the glass-maker that many were made commercially. Examples of glass toys would be an unusual addition to a comprehensive toy collection, but the search for them needs a keen eye because they are not all obviously toys.

Glass was, and still is, used as part of other toys – the turning glass rod of the automata waterfalls, the windows and light fittings of old dolls' houses and the eyes for dolls. In 1824, a Birmingham manufacturer speaking before the House of Commons stated that he had received an order for £500 worth of dolls' eyes – a considerable sum in today's currency.

Street traders also made glass eyes for humans and for dolls. Henry Mayhew in his *London Labour & the London Poor* (1851), tells us something of this extraordinary trade: two types were made for dolls – the common and the natural. The common variety were simply small hollow glass spheres made of white enamel and coloured either black or blue; the 'bettermost' dolls' eyes, or the natural ones, were made after the same fashion, but in a superior manner (this same trader supplied glass eyes at half the price to servants saying 'false eyes are a great charity to servants. If they lose an eye no-one will engage them').

In England, famous localities for glass production were Stourbridge, Newcastle, Birmingham, London and Bristol. Workers from the old glass houses still tell of the amusing trifles a man would make and take home for his family. Various shapes might take his fancy – a thimble, a tiny glass book (always a bible), a glass sow with piglets, a swan or a fish. These imaginative 'one-off' piece were called 'Friggers' and on Mayday, when children marched through the streets, many a father would make a glass trumpet for his children.

The glass baubles used for decoration at Christmas, so delicate and beautiful, had to be handled with great care. Most were imported to England and were attached by metal loops to tree or light fitting. Shapes

Below

At top, a set of blue glass miniatures. Although similar sets were made for dolls' houses, most examples were travellers' samples which could be carried with ease and safety.

Victorian/English/Size: jug 1in

Below, tiny candlesticks and glass birds in cages. These were typical examples of 'Friggers', called 'Whimsies' in America. The elaborate decoration on these small take-home pieces indicates that they were never made commercially.

Victorian/English/Size: 1in

were many and varied: small and large glass balls, brilliant glass birds with spun tails, circlets of coloured glass beads, replicas of Father Christmas, and many others. Perhaps their fragility ensured their survival – children are surprisingly careful of what they realise is precious.

Snowstorms and Gulls. The landscapes with falling snow, precipitated by a turn of the wrist, resembled hollow paper-weights. Some contained Christmas scenes and others showed farm buildings or local landmarks. The minute flecks descending on seascapes were intended to represent gulls and, like the glass lighthouses or bells filled with coloured sand, were mainly for the souvenir toy trade.

Various examples of glass decorations for Christmas. The bird has a spun glass tail and this part was often made by young boys at home, wishing to earn extra pocket money. Below centre, marbles. The older and cheaper variety were of stone, the oldest probably of baked clay, but it was the veined and gloriously coloured glass marbles that every child longed to own. They made up their own games, many of them with traditional rules, but the size and the gay spiral pattern of the marble was the great attraction. Fine marbles were known as 'taws' and 'alleys' – the latter perhaps a contraction of alabaster, from which they were originally made. Marbles were sometimes played indoors and were also used as components of other games (solitaire), but they were chiefly a boys' game for city streets. The engine, gun and monkey are moulded glass sweet containers. Glass containers of all sorts were manufactured – glass hats, lanterns, pipes, boats etc – and remained as toys or ornaments. For display, they were usually filled with 'hundreds and thousands', cachous, or small sweets. American collectors of glass novelties are especially fortunate because the manufacture of these amusing trifles was particularly prolific in the United States. Mary Louise Stanley, in her book *A Century of Glass Toys*, lists well over 1,000 examples.

The Butcher, The Baker, The Candlestick Maker

An unusual sideline for toy collectors could be a section devoted to occupations. During the Victorian era, when home dressmaking for dolls was a popular nursery pastime, many variations were made upon the more common 'little girl' and 'baby' themes. Most upper and middle class Victorian households had servants (wages were low by present standards and employment for women without much education had to be in the domestic sphere). A closer look at the structure of a Victorian family gives some idea of what could be available for the collector today. Dolls representing mother, father, grandparents, bride and bridegroom are easily found and although these must be considered as relationships rather than as occupations, they have a rightful place in a specialist collection. The household itself presents great scope, with the nanny and governess installed in the nursery and the cook ruling the kitchen, helped or hindered by maids of varying importance in the hierarchy 'below stairs'. In the towns, the outside staff was minimal, but a gardener, coachman and stable-boy were considered normal for a middle class country home.

When the family went on holiday, all sorts of souvenir toys might be purchased: gypsies, stall-holders, bazaar-sellers, Punch and

Maid with German bisque head on stuffed and weighted body; probably used as a door-stop. Dressed as a parlourmaid in black dress, white apron with bib.

c 1890/Height: 15in

Schoolboy; German bisque head with composition limbs, and dressed as an English schoolboy of the turn of the century with brown peaked cap, breeches and jacket, flannel waistcoat, stiff white collar and red bow tie.

Height: 12in

Gypsy pedlar; papier mâché head on stuffed base. Her basket holds beads, small dolls, paper books, pins, buttons etc. Dressed in blue dress, white apron and red cloak.

c 1855/English/Height: 13in

Judy and perhaps a fisherman made of shells stuck to a wooden doll – decoration with shells was a popular Victorian craft. Travellers from abroad brought home special dolls dressed in national costume and these often represented occupations – fishermen from Brittany, lace-makers from Brussels, dancers from Spain and cowboys from America. Some collectors specialise in 'costume' or 'national' dolls. The earlier ones were of bisque or china; modern examples are of composition or plastic.

In some English country districts, wares were still hawked from door to door, so a pedlar woman with minute wares stuck to her tray, or clustered in her basket, was frequently assembled at home. A rare inventory concerning a 'petty chapman' or pedlar of 1658 lists a fascinating variety of wares including: 'remnants of lawn, Holland and Callico, buckskyn gloves, fyne ribbon and Ferritt ribbon, shell rings, silver seales and thimbles, spectacles, small lace and dressings, taffety and tiffany hoods, ivory combs, scissers, pins, bandstrings and fancyes'.

Hunting was enjoyed by many well-to-do country families and figures were dressed as riders in hunting 'pink' (actually bright red). In the streets a child could see a hurdy-gurdy man and often a policeman standing at the top of the area steps chatting and having a cup of tea with the cook. Perhaps the housemaid had a 'follower' – as boy friends were called in those days – a soldier or sailor home on leave? High days and holidays sometimes brought an invitation to the theatre or concert and could mean a doll dressed as an admired performer. Indeed, dolls representing notable artists from the world of entertainment have always found buyers – Taglioni in paper with hand-coloured costumes, Jenny Lind, Dolly Varden, the Gibson Girl, Charlie Chaplin, etc.

A call at the shops with Mama meant a biscuit from the grocer and, if a new bonnet was needed, an exciting glimpse of the world of fashion at the milliner's shop. In the streets, a postman could be seen pulling his hand-cart, and treats such as a visit to the circus were remembered by dressing a doll as a clown or acrobat. Religious instruction was never neglected and dolls can be found robed as nuns, clergymen and Quakers. There were even toys for teaching the ritual of the Mass with small replicas of altars and candlesticks accompanied by figures of priests and servers, and Christmas, of course, was the time for Santa Claus and fairy dolls.

The possibilities are intriguing. In addition to the dolls especially dressed, there were figures as witches, fortune-tellers, bootblacks, musicians, footballers, hikers, swimmers and so on. Grand and humble occupations were represented in the toy world. Statesmen, admirals and field marshalls shared the stage with postmen, railway porters, sweeps and cobblers, and to a toy collector all are welcome. Some old home-made toys are worth preserving. The faces and features may be primitive, but the style and fabric of the clothes are usually correct for the period. There should also be an honoured place for special 'types' – the frontier Indian and the 'Mammy' dolls of a bygone era.

It must be remembered that in those days people were required to dress according to their station; uniforms were worn by indoor

Left
A fishergirl with bisque head, stuffed body and composition limbs; dressed in traditional costume and carrying a shrimping net and cockle basket. Made for the souvenir trade.

c 1900/French/Height: 12½ in

Organ grinder; composition head with painted features, peg leg and steel hook for one hand; the figure represents a sailor from the battle of Trafalgar. As the music plays, one hand turns the handle of the small slung musical box and the head nods. Dressed in cloth breeches and black coat.

English/Height: 11in

Right
Religieuse; wax head and arms, with pupilless glass eyes. Dressed in fawn linen with paper lining.

c 1850/French/Height: 8in

Priest; wax head and wooden limbs, with pupilless glass eyes. Vestments of cream, black and red silk.

c 1870/Italian/Height: 9in

and outdoor staff. Professional men, clerks and schoolboys wore stiff white collars; little girls' dresses were protected by pinafores. The 'quality' – the upper classes – had innumerable hat styles for different occasions, whilst the working man was typified by his muffler and cloth cap.

Today even the traditionally blackened figure of the sweep is on his way out, and since the corner store has been replaced by the supermarket we seldom see a fishmonger in his straw hat, a butcher in his striped apron, or a shop assistant, resplendent in frock-coat, attending personally to his customers.

Many collections show dolls of different materials, makers and ages, but few specialise in presenting a way of life now vanished. Many occupations can be found depicted in the large selection of tin toys of the 1880s and 1890s – these represent in miniature the transport and everyday life of that bustling period. The figures should wear their original clothing, or at least enough of it to show their occupation. It may not be possible to keep to scale in a collection of this sort but, just as a wax doll,

Laurel and Hardy; two portrait dolls of stuffed fabric with painted features, representing the popular American film comics. The dolls are free-standing and dressed in coloured felt.

c 1925-1935/American/Height: 12½in

Hunting party, mounted on the original selling card and comprising five bisque-headed dolls with painted features and hair wigs; bodies and limbs of rolled, stuffed paper. Dressed in black, cream and red crêpe paper.

c 1910/English/Height: 5½in

complete with original underclothes shows us the stays, bodices, petticoats etc favoured by our great-grandmothers, so the grouping together of the occupations and vocations of the past presents an informative picture, not only of the ingenuity of the toy manufacturers and dressmakers, but also of the social conditions of life as it was lived many years ago.

A specialist 'occupational' collection could be widened to include portrait dolls resembling royalty, statesmen, celebrities, soldiers, artists and characters from children's books. Fashions change rapidly and appreciation should not depend upon antiquity. A collector should not disregard the seemingly inconsequential: the little celluloid baseball player, the twenties 'flapper' with no waist and a bandeau round her bob, the astronaut or small space-traveller – these are easily regarded as commonplace, until accumulating age and rarity transforms them into antiques – at three times the price!

Just as the china manufacturers copied famous (and notorious) characters as ornaments, similarly dolls were dressed and toys were made to commemorate important events and people. A bonus to this fascinating study is the fact that the rarity – and thus the expense – of the toy's origin is unimportant. For the collector who seeks the occupation and not the maker, the toy representing an authentic and perhaps uncommon or vanishing occupation is a greater prize than the rarest Bru doll.

Occupations, great or humble, are universal, and each country is distinguished by its own personalities and literature. America has a unique culture, and counterparts for most of those vocations described here. They march through the centuries and before our eyes – but do we see them? Perhaps our gaze is transfixed by wonderful waxes and beautiful bisques, and we miss those irreplaceable, sometimes shabby items which mark our present history.

A portrait doll of Field Marshal Earl Kitchener of Khartoum, with cloth body, composition limbs and head with painted features and moulded moustache. Dressed in British army uniform of khaki breeches, puttees and high-collared jacket.

Early 1900s/British/Height: 18½in

Histories

To encourage collectors to explore and record the history of their acquisitions, here are stories to illustrate the rewards of research.

The Cadbury Dolls In 1794 Richard Tapper Cadbury settled in Birmingham, England, and established himself as a silk mercer. One of his sons, Joel, went to America in 1815 where he prospered, married and raised a family.

In 1831-32 Joel returned to England and carried with him a gift for his mother of three dolls dressed by his wife Caroline to represent his three eldest children. This gift was mentioned by his daughter Mary, when she was eight years old, in a letter written from Philadelphia to her grandmother in 1831.

My Dear Grandmother,

I hope thee is well. I am now ready to send thee a doll of this country and I hope thee will be pleased with them and they are dressed just like brother john an Myself, richard and john likes To little joel is thee sweetest little fellow – he is so good he never cries little elisabeth is very good too. Richard and john and myself goes to school and learns geography and defention and I hope thee will be pleased with my letter for this is the very first that I have written and mother said that it was done very well but I had made some mistake in writing.

I am very much oblige to thee for that letter it is very pretty and I hope thee will write me another very soon.

I remain thy affectionate granddaughter
Mary Ann Cadbury.
9 mo 19 1831.

Two papier mâché dolls dressed as Quaker children. The girl has moulded black hair, highly coloured cheeks and blue eyes; the arms and hands are of wood. She wears a long striped dress with cotton pinafore and shoulder cape; her deep straw bonnet is silk lined and she wears mittens on her arms. The boy is a similar type of doll and he wears long fawn trousers and short jacket – the trousers button at the side and the jacket at the front. He wears a frilled collar and trimmed straw hat.

c 1831/American

The miller's doll, made of wood, with jointed legs and kid forearms. The gessoed wooden head has painted features and blue eyes with pupils. She wears cotton pantaloons and petticoat beneath the cream organza dress.
Georgiana kept the doll carefully all her life and handed it on to her descendants, still safe in its shell casket. And so it has remained with even the elegant mohair wig still coiffeurred in the original style and adorned with artificial flowers.

c 1795-1805/English/Height: doll 21½in

In the 1860s two of the dolls were returned to America and in 1931 (100 years after Mary Ann's letter) they were stored away in one of the oldest houses in Moorestown, New Jersey.

Quakers, however, are good record-keepers and the existence of the dolls was known. Possessions were sorted and at last the hunt moved to the attic. Frustrated and exhausted, the searchers turned to a pile of old boxes and began to unpack them. In the very bottom box were the missing dolls and the original letter from Mary Ann.

The Miller's Doll In the mid-nineteenth century, a prosperous miller and his family were living in Suffolk. His daughter Georgiana was born in 1848.

The miller, however, had one customer who was unable to pay his debts and this client asked the miller to accept a beautiful doll as part payment. The miller agreed,

thinking of Georgiana, and so she received this doll as a present in about 1852. It was already an heirloom when she received it.

But the story is not over. It was decided to make a shell house for the doll; the inside walls were prettily papered and the whole gift sealed – almost hermetically – which was frustrating for Georgiana, but a blessing for posterity.

The Gladstone Bazaar Stall The bazaar stall and doll belonged to Mrs. Stephen Gladstone, daughter-in-law of Prime Minister William Ewart Gladstone, which probably dates them to about the middle of the nineteenth century. The Gladstones lived at Hawarden Castle, Flintshire, which originally belonged to the Derby family, the Stanleys, whose estates were confiscated by Oliver Cromwell and sold to one of the Gladstone ancestors.

Left
The bazaar stall; the miniature wares include tiny peg-wooden dolls, stationery with quills, clergyman's 'bands', woven braces, shoes, sewing set and feather dusters. The doll has a wax head and arms on a wooden body and is dressed in fragile silk with lace overskirt.

c 1840-1850/English/Height: stall 10½in

Hints for Collectors

For all collectors there is one cardinal rule – catalogue everything, no matter how small. Each item should have a number attached and a corresponding number entered in the record with the following information:

Detailed description
Date or period of origin
Date and price of purchase
From whom or where purchased
If there is a history acquired with the object, number this similarly and file with the original entry.

If you have space enough, you can gather examples of most types of playthings. If space is limited, it may be better to specialise – eg dolls or dolls' houses; model soldiers or tin toys; pull-along toys or automata. No matter which field you choose, a library of reference books particular to your chosen subject is essential. It can be built up slowly, as the specialist books come out, but it will prove invaluable and, eventually, your research may enable you to add to existing knowledge.

Display

Again, space has to be the deciding factor. Sufficient room enables you to provide cabinets, etc. If you have little space, an alcove – even a bookcase fitted with adjustable shelves – will suffice. A sheet of perspex to front the shelves is much better and lighter than glass.

Many toys are free-standing and present no problems, but dolls are better displayed standing up and if you cannot obtain special stands for them, excellent results can be obtained by standing them in large jam/coffee jars. These are secure, with a broad base, and the skirts of the antique doll pull down over the jar, covering it completely. This method also enables you to put a little anti-moth preparation into the base. Remember that if you are dealing with wax items, a controlled temperature is ideal and strong sunlight must be avoided.

Large items that do not need close study can be displayed high up, thus keeping your valuable eye-level space for those that need inspection. Glass domes are most useful since covered objects can be kept free of dust and moth damage, and they also enable you to free valuable cabinet space.

Labelling

Whatever system you employ, the label must be readable at a fair distance without spectacles. It should be placed near each item and give the maximum of information to the viewer without 'overloading' the display.

An alternative method, if the display is not changed often, is to number each item and affix a card adjacent to the cabinet or shelf with the numbers listed thereon and relevant information given.

Security

A valuable collection merits the protection afforded by special locks, alarm systems and adequate insurance. Expensive pieces should be priced, photographed and separately insured. Do not keep your records and insurance documents in the same place as your exhibition. If you are unlucky enough to lose all or part of your collection, you will have fully documented evidence to produce if required.

Storage

Cupboards beneath cabinets or shelves are ideal for storage. Labelled boxes containing smaller items can be stacked until needed to change a display, and objects likely to rust should be lightly oiled. It is important that all items are catalogued and numbered before being stored and that precautions are taken against moth damage. Dolls with fixed or movable eyes should be stored face downwards.

Restoration

This is a subject upon which the experts differ, but most agree that items on display are better shown as near as possible to their original condition. However, a dated record of any major restoration should be filed with the catalogue information. Valuable items, some textiles and difficult wax repairs should be left to the professional restorer.

Building up a collection

The good piece finds its own market price, whether one buys privately, through dealers, or in sale rooms. Happily we all find bargains from time to time and there is the friendly custom of swapping with other collectors. However modest a collection may be to begin with, sooner or later a better example is acquired and the second best is exchanged. This is how collections are built and is one of the best methods if there is limited money available.

There are societies for specific types of collecting, membership of which facilitates the exchange of news and helpful hints, as well as the exchange of duplicates. American and European clubs sometimes offer overseas membership and collectors are advised to join these when possible.

The camera is most useful to collectors, since a small print of the item to be considered for exchange or sale enables all the preliminary assessment to be done by post.

Summary Your collection should be catalogued in detail, displayed to advantage, secured against theft and damage, restored truthfully, and built up with knowledge and care.

Bibliography

Baecker und Haas, *Die Anderen Nurnberger* (Hobby Haas, Frankfurt 1973)

Barenholtz, Edith F. (ed). *The George Brown Toy Sketchbook* (The Pyne Press 1971)

Bell, R. C. *Board and Table Games* (OUP 1960)

Buday, George. *The History of the Christmas Card* (Rockliff Publishing Corporation 1954)

Cain, John. *Talking Machines* (Methuen 1961)

Chapuis, A. & Droz, E. *Automata* (Neuchatel 1958)

Coleman, Dorothy, Elizabeth & Evelyn. *The Collector's Encyclopaedia of Dolls* (Crown Publishers, New York 1968)

Cries of London

Cunnington, P. & Buck, Anne. *Children's Costume in England 1300-1900* (A. & C. Black 1965)

Daiken, Leslie. *Children's Toys throughout the Ages* (Batsford 1953)

Davis, Dorothy. *A History of Shopping* (Routledge and Kegan Paul 1966)

Delgardo, Alan. *Victorian Entertainment* (David & Charles 1971)

Desmonde, Kay. *All Colour Book of Dolls* (Octopus Books 1974)

Early, Alice K. *English Dolls, Effigies and Puppets* (Batsford 1955)

Fawcett, Clara Hallard. *Dolls, A New Guide for Collectors* (Charles Branford, Boston 1965)

Fraser, Antonia. *A History of Toys* (Weidenfeld & Nicolson 1966)

Fritzsch, Karl E. & Bachmann, Manfred. *An Illustrated History of Toys* (Abbey Library 1966)

Gerken, Jo Elizabeth. *Wonderful Dolls of Wax* (Doll Research Associates, Lincoln, Nebraska 1964)

Gordon, Lesley. *Peepshow into Paradise—A History Of Children's Toys* (Harrap 1953)

Greene, Vivien. *English Dolls' Houses of the Eighteenth and Nineteenth Centuries* (Batsford 1955)

Harris, Henry. *Model Soldiers* (Weidenfeld & Nicolson 1962)

Hertz, Louis H. *The Toy Collector* (Funk & Wagnalls, New York 1969)

Hillier, Mary, *Dolls & Dollmakers* (Weidenfeld & Nicolson 1968)

Hillier, Mary. *Pageant of Toys* (Elek Books 1965)

Huggett, Frank E. *A Day in the Life of a Victorian Farm Worker* (George Allen & Unwin 1972)

Jacobs, Flora Gill & Faurholt, Estrid. *Dolls & Doll Houses* (Charles E. Tuttle 1967)

Jacobs, Flora Gill. *A History of Dolls' Houses* (Charles Scribner's Sons 1965)

Jendrick, Barbara Whitton. *Paper Dolls & Paper Toys of Raphael Tuck & Sons* (Jendrick, 1970)

Lambeth, M. *A New Golden Dolly* (The Cornucopia Press 1966)

Latham, J. *Dolls' Houses* (A. & C. Black 1969)

Longman, E. D. & Loch, S. *Pins and Pincushions* (Longmans, Green 1911)

Low, Frances H. *Queen Victoria's Dolls* (Geo Newnes 1894)

Maddison, John. *Living Pictures* (Penguin Books 1950)

Maingot, Eliane. *Les Automates* (Hachette 1959)

Manley, C. C. *Collectible Glass—Book 4, British Glass* (T. & V. Lagerberg 1968)

McClinton, Katharine Morrison. *Antiques of American Childhood* (Bramhall House 1970)

Muir, Percy. *English Children's Books, 1600-1900* (Batsford 1954)

Murray, Patrick. *Toys* (Studio Vista/Dutton 1968)

Noble, John. *Dolls* (Studio Vista 1967)

Ord-Hume, Arthur W. J. G. *Clockwork Music* (George Allen & Unwin 1973)

Pearsall, Ronald. *Collecting Mechanical Antiques* (David & Charles 1973)

Perry, Evan. *Collecting Antique Metalware* (Country Life Books 1974)

Polkinghorne, R. K. & M. I. R. *Toy-making in School & Home* (Harrap & Co 1917)

Prasteau, Jean. *Les Automates* (Grund, Paris 1968)

Quennell, Marjorie & C. H. B. *A History of Everyday Things in England* (Batsford 1919)

Quennell, Peter (ed). *Mayhew's London* (Hamlyn 1969)

Quennell, Peter (ed). *Mayhew's Characters* (Hamlyn 1969)

Rabecq-Maillard, M-M. *Histoire du Jouet* (Hachette 1962)

Remise, Jac & Fondin, Jean. *The Golden Age of Toys* (Edita Lausanne, trans. T. B. Tubbs, Patrick Stephens 1967)

Richards, L. W. *Old British Model Soldiers 1893-1918* (Arms & Armour Press 1970)

Speaight, George. *The History of the English Toy Theatre* (Studio Vista 1969)

Stanley, Mary Louise. *A Century of Glass Toys* (Forward's Colour Productions)

St George, Eleanor. *The Dolls of Yesterday* (Charles Scribner's Sons 1948)

Taylor, Arthur. *Discovering Model Soldiers* (Shire Publications, Tring 1970)

Temple, Nigel. *Seen and Not Heard* (Hutchinson 1970)

Toller, Jane. *Antique Miniature Furniture in Great Britain and America* (G. Bell & Sons 1966)

Toller, Jane. *Regency & Victorian Crafts* (Ward Lock 1969)

White, Gwen. *Antique Toys & Their Background* (Batsford 1971)

White, Gwen. *European & American Dolls* (Batsford 1966)

Whitehouse, F. R. B. *Table Games of Georgian and Victorian Days* (Priory Press & Chad Valley 1971)

Museum Publications

Cultural Ctte of Corporation of Manchester. *Fashion in Miniature—Gallery of English Costume* (1970)

HMSO. *Toys and Games—London Museum* (1963)

Musée d'Histoire. *Les Automates des Jaquet-Droz*

Scott-Kemball, Jeune, Trustees of the British Museum. *Javanese Shadow Puppets* (1970)

Simmons, T. M. *Railways—to the end of the Nineteenth Century* (HMSO 1964)

Thomas, D. B. *The Origins of the Motion Picture* (HMSO 1964)

Victoria & Albert Museum. *Seasons Greetings* (1971)

Westcott, G. F. *The British Railway Locomotive 1803-1853* (HMSO 1958)

Catalogues and Trade Papers

Bassett-Lowke Railways Ltd. *Bassett-Lowke railways* (1968)

British Toymaker, The, 1915-1916 (20 parts)

J. Theobald & Co. *Catalogue of Conjuring Apparatus* (1884)

Index